THE 5 IN 10 CHICKEN BREAST COOKBOOK

5 Ingredients in 10 Minutes or Less

MELANIE BARNARD
AND BROOKE DOJNY

A JOHN BOSWELL ASSOCIATES / KING HILL PRODUCTIONS BOOK

HEARST BOOKS

NEW YORK

It is the policy of William Morrow and Company, Inc., and its imprints and affiliates, recognizing the importance of preserving what has been written, to print the books we publish on acid-free paper, and we exert our best efforts to that end.

Library of Congress Cataloging-in-Publication Data

Barnard, Melanie.
    The 5 in 10 chicken breast cookbook : 5 ingredients in 10 minutes
or less / Melanie Barnard and Brooke Dojny.
        p.   cm.
    "A John Boswell Associates/King Hill Productions book."
    Includes index.
    ISBN 0-688-12689-8
    1. Cookery (Chicken)   2. Quick and easy cookery.   I. Dojny,
Brooke.   II. Title.   III. Title: Five in ten chicken breast
cookbook.
    TX750.5.C45B37   1993
    641.6'65—dc20   93-14270
                                                                            CIP

Printed in the United States of America

First Edition

1   2   3   4   5   6   7   8   9   10

Book design by Barbara Cohen Aronica

CONTENTS

Each one is a meal in a bowl, with exciting flavors, such as Spring Chicken Soup with Asparagus and Egg Noodles, Chicken and White Bean Soup with Pesto and Chicken Tortilla Soup.

Warming and wonderful, these easy recipes range from homey Quick Chicken and Dumplings and Spicy Chicken Chili to high-style Coq au Vin and Moroccan Chicken with Apricots and Couscous.

Sautéed Chicken with Bananas and Rum, Garlic Chicken with Balsamic Vinegar and Brandied Chicken au Poivre are just a few of the one-pan ideas you'll find in this chapter.

4. STIR-FRIES 77

Incredible variety and an exciting mix of flavors—Peanut Chicken Stir-Fry, Lemon Chicken with Green Onions, Ginger Chicken and Mixed Vegetables—are stirred up in a flash.

5. BAKED AND BROILED 89

Broiled Buffalo Chicken, just like the famous wings, Broiled Peachy Chicken and Baked Chicken Italiano are a few of the oven-cooked recipes that make the most of skinless, boneless chicken breasts.

6. BARBECUES AND GRILLS 104

Chicken breasts are just as good outdoors as in, as illustrated by recipes like Orange and Honey Grilled Chicken, Grilled Chicken with Pineapple Salsa, Indonesian Chicken Satay and Grilled Chicken with Lemon and Fennel Butter.

7. HOT AND COLD SALADS 130

Chicken goes light in tempting salads for all seasons: Caesar Chicken Salad, Chicken Antipasto and Chicken Taco Salad are just a few examples.

INTRODUCTION

We wonder if most young children have any inkling that chicken meat comes under a skin and attached to bones—let alone know what a whole bird looks like. The butcher who first cut the meat off a chicken breast and wrapped it in a package really was a genius. Little did he know that we'd all be more than willing to pay for the privilege of not having to deal with all those inconvenient bones and skin.

Chicken has long been a best-seller in the supermarket meat case, but lately America's favorite bird (and its various parts) have just about taken over. Store-prepared boneless, skinless breasts enjoy a huge share of that market. The reasons are obvious: they are quick, easy, lower in fat than many other cuts and, pound for pound of meat, relatively inexpensive. We recognize all these attributes, but especially love them for another quality—versatility. Chicken breasts are mildly flavored, tender and juicy, which makes them an appealing basis for almost unlimited variations. In fact, 167 of them follow in this book.

Developing these recipes has been a pleasant challenge. We broiled, sautéed, baked, braised, grilled and stir-fried. Then we made soups, salads and sandwiches. Every time, the chicken came through for delicious, attractive main courses that we, our families and our friends devoured happily night after night.

We've enjoyed exploring some new and improved convenience ingredients, such as internationally flavored stewed tomatoes, quick-cooking white and brown rice, canned reduced-sodium chicken broth, frozen vegetable combinations, good-quality salsas, pasta sauces, pesto, salad dressings, prepared pizza shells and garlic bread, and grated cheeses. In addition, all sorts of pre-trimmed and ready-cut fruits and vegetables, from broccoli to melons to pineapple, are appearing in both the produce section and the salad bar of many large supermarkets. We took full advantage of all of them in developing these 5 in 10 recipes: easy-to-prepare dishes that are made with just 5 ingredients—not counting salt and pepper—and that cook in 10 minutes or less.

We found that when only a few ingredients are used in a dish, both quality and quantity mean a lot. Whether it is an in-season vine-ripened tomato or a can of seasoned stewed tomatoes, buying the best gives true, clear flavors. Similarly, making a big hit with a single seasoning (whether it's fresh basil, chopped garlic or even black pepper), turns a ho-hum recipe into a memorable main dish.

Proper cooking and handling of chicken is important in order to guard against the risk of salmonella. Salmonella bacteria are killed with heat, so any poultry cooked to an internal temperature of 180 degrees F. is safe. But because skinless, boneless chicken breasts are relatively thin, a meat thermometer is difficult to use, so other tests are easier and more accurate. Properly cooked chicken will be white throughout, with no traces of pink, and the juices will run clear golden rather than red when pricked with a knife point.

The greater danger for salmonella contamination is careless cleaning of kitchen surfaces and tools. Cutting boards, platters and knives used in working with raw chicken should be thoroughly washed in very hot, soapy water immediately after use. Finally, leftover cooked chicken should not be left at room temperature, but should be refrigerated as soon as possible.

As far is timing is concerned, chicken breasts really do cook in 10 minutes or less, particularly if they're slightly flattened or cut into various smaller shapes and sizes. We often suggest that the meat be cut into a particular size of cubes, chunks or pieces. These measurements are approximate; no need to get out the ruler! But they do give you an idea of size. Cooking times are always approximate, too, but other than calling for preheating an oven or a grill, actual cooking should take place in the time allotted.

We hope that you will use this book as a springboard for your own ideas and variations. Just remember to keep it as quick and simple as 1, 2, 3, 4, 5.

1 Soups and Chowders

Chicken soup, for so long that quintessential cure-all comfort food, has emerged from the era when it required long hours of attention into the sphere of the 5 in 10 cook. And most welcome it is, too, for the restorative qualities of chicken soup are renowned and genuine. Good-quality canned chicken broth is what has made the most difference, with a couple of excellent national brands leading the way. Reduced-sodium chicken broth is also widely marketed.

Canned stewed tomatoes are another terrific boon to quick soup making. These days, they come in different flavors tailored with international seasonings, such as Italian and Mexican style as well as the classic "original." It helps if you can find chopped stewed tomatoes as opposed to the bulkier sliced variety.

All of these soup recipes call for the chicken meat to be cut into small cubes or thin strips. If you're working with chicken breasts, you might find it easiest to partly freeze each breast and then cut in half *horizontally* first before cutting the pieces or slices.

Although we've written most of these recipes to serve four to six people, the only 5 in 10 limitation to making larger quantities is in the time it takes for the liquid to come to a boil. So since soup is always a wonderful crowd-pleaser, by all means consider making larger pots of any of these recipes if you have the extra time.

CHICKEN AVGOLEMONO

3/4 pound skinless, boneless chicken breasts
2 lemons
5 cups chicken broth
1 cup quick-cooking rice
3 eggs
　　Salt and freshly ground pepper

1. Cut the chicken crosswise on a slight diagonal into thin slices. Grate 1 teaspoon of the colored zest and squeeze 1/4 cup juice from the lemons.

2. In a large nonreactive saucepan, combine the chicken broth with 2 cups water. Bring to a boil over high heat. Add the chicken slices, reduce the heat to medium-low and simmer for 2 minutes. Add the rice, cover and cook for 4 minutes. Reduce the heat to low.

3. In a medium heatproof bowl, whisk the eggs with the lemon zest and lemon juice until blended. Slowly whisk 1 cup of the hot soup liquid into the eggs. Then whisk the eggs into the remaining soup in the pot.

4. Cook, stirring constantly, until all is hot and the soup is thickened very slightly by the eggs, 1 to 2 minutes. Do not boil or the eggs will curdle. Season with salt and pepper to taste and serve at once.

3 TO 4 SERVINGS

CHICKEN "BOUILLABAISSE"

Fennel, saffron and garlic lend this tomato-based chicken soup some of the characteristic flavors of a Mediterranean bouillabaisse. To add even more authenticity, toast slices of French bread, spread with mayonnaise spiked with cayenne pepper and float on top of each serving of soup.

1 pound skinless, boneless chicken breasts
1 medium fennel bulb
2 cans (14 to 16 ounces) Italian-style stewed tomatoes
3/4 teaspoon crushed saffron threads
2 teaspoons bottled chopped garlic in oil
  Salt and freshly ground pepper

1. Cut the chicken into 3/4-inch cubes. Trim the fennel, halve lengthwise and cut into thin slices.

2. In a large nonreactive saucepan, combine the tomatoes with their juices, the fennel and 4 cups of water. Cover the saucepan and bring to a boil over high heat. Boil for 2 minutes.

3. Add the chicken and saffron threads to the soup, reduce the heat to medium and simmer, uncovered, until the chicken is white but still moist in the center, about 5 minutes. Stir in the garlic in oil and season with salt and pepper to taste.

4 TO 6 SERVINGS

CHINESE CHICKEN NOODLE SOUP

Crispy fried noodles, sometimes called fried wontons, add crunch and flavor to this simple Chinese chicken soup. These are usually sold in cans in the Asian foods sections of supermarkets.

3/4 pound skinless, boneless chicken breasts
8 green onions
6 cups chicken broth
2 tablespoons soy sauce
    Freshly ground pepper
2 cups crispy fried Chinese noodles

1. Cut the chicken breasts into thin slivers. Thinly slice the green onions.

2. In a large saucepan or soup pot, combine the broth with 2 cups water. Bring to a boil over high heat. Reduce the heat to medium-low and add the chicken. Immediately cover the pot and cook until the chicken is white but still moist in the center, 3 to 4 minutes.

3. Stir the green onions and soy sauce into the soup. Season with pepper to taste. Ladle into bowls and top each portion with 1/3 to 1/2 cup fried noodles.

4 TO 6 SERVINGS

CREAMY CHICKEN CHOWDER

We love the satisfying heartiness of potato-rich chowders, and so were delighted to find that pre-cooked and diced frozen hash brown potatoes could be used to make this simply fabulous chicken chowder in the 10-minute time allotment. Pilot biscuits or common crackers are the traditional accompaniment, along with a big salad of leafy greens.

3/4 pound skinless, boneless chicken breasts
1 tablespoon poultry seasoning
8 green onions
4 cups half-and-half
1 pound (about 4 cups) frozen hash brown potatoes
1 teaspoon salt
1/4 teaspoon freshly ground pepper

1. Cut the chicken into 1/2-inch cubes. Toss with the poultry seasoning to season on all sides. Finely chop the green onions.

2. In a large saucepan or soup pot, combine the half-and-half, 1 cup water and the frozen potatoes. Bring to a boil over high heat, stirring to break up the potatoes.

3. Add the chicken to the soup pot, cover and cook over medium-low heat until the potatoes are tender, about 8 minutes. Stir in the green onions and season with the salt and pepper.

3 TO 4 SERVINGS

Chicken Escarole Soup

Escarole is a flavorful, pleasantly bitter green that's wonderful in soup. This one is the essence of delicious Italian simplicity, with just a bit of garlic and Parmesan cheese stirred in at the end.

1 pound escarole
3/4 pound skinless, boneless chicken breasts
5 cups chicken broth
1 1/2 teaspoons bottled chopped garlic in oil
1/2 cup grated Parmesan cheese
Freshly ground pepper

1. Cut the escarole leaves crosswise into 1/2-inch-wide shreds. Cut the chicken breasts into thin strips.

2. In a large saucepan or soup pot, combine the chicken broth with 3 cups of water. Cover and bring to a boil over high heat. When the broth boils, add the chicken and stir in the escarole. Reduce the heat to medium-low and simmer, partly covered, until the chicken is white but still moist in the center and the escarole is tender, 5 to 7 minutes.

3. Remove the soup from the heat and stir in the garlic in oil and the Parmesan cheese. Season generously with pepper.

3 TO 4 SERVINGS

HEARTY CHICKEN AND WINTER VEGETABLE SOUP

We recommend taking full advantage of all the wonderful frozen vegetable combinations now appearing in the supermarket. Most of them taste just great, and they are a real convenience food when you consider that all you do is simply open the package and measure them out. This commonly available combination of carrots, onions and celery is especially nice to add to a hearty chicken and pasta soup.

6 cups chicken broth
3 cups frozen mixed soup vegetables (carrots, onions, celery)
1 cup tubettini or ditalini, or other small pasta (about 4 ounces)
3/4 pound skinless, boneless chicken breasts
2 teaspoons Italian seasoning
Salt and freshly ground pepper

1. In a large saucepan or soup pot, combine the chicken broth, 2 cups water, the frozen vegetables and the pasta. Cover and bring to a boil over high heat, stirring occasionally.

2. Meanwhile, cut the chicken into 1/2-inch-wide slices. Add to the pot along with the Italian seasoning. Partially cover and cook over medium-low heat until the pasta is tender and the chicken is white but still moist in the center, 6 to 8 minutes. Season with salt and pepper to taste.

4 TO 5 SERVINGS

CHICKEN PASTINA EN BRODO

The original Italian "comfort soup," *pastina en brodo* is the perfect antidote to almost any problem, from a chest cold to a difficult day at the office. Egg pastina (tiny star-shaped pasta) is available in most supermarkets, but if you can't find it, orzo or tubetti—or even pasta alphabets—can be substituted.

3/4 pound skinless, boneless chicken breasts
 2 slender carrots
 6 cups chicken broth
3/4 cup egg pastina (4 ounces)
1/2 cup grated Parmesan cheese
    Freshly ground pepper

1. Cut the chicken into 1/2-inch cubes. Peel the carrots and cut into thin slices.

2. In a large saucepan or soup pot, combine the chicken broth, sliced carrots and 2 cups water. Cover the saucepan and bring to a boil over high heat. Cook for 2 minutes.

3. Add the chicken and pastina to the soup. Reduce the heat to medium-low and continue to cook, covered, until the carrots and pastina are tender and the chicken is white but still moist in the center, about 5 minutes.

4. Stir in the Parmesan cheese and season with pepper to taste.

4 TO 5 SERVINGS

SPINACH NOODLE CHICKEN SOUP

While it takes more preparation time, you could also use 1 pound of chopped fresh spinach instead of frozen in this beautiful green soup. Look for washed, ready-to-use spinach leaves. And if you can't find spinach noodles, you can certainly substitute regular egg noodles. This is a hearty dish that is a meal in a bowl.

6 cups chicken broth
1 package (10 ounces) frozen chopped spinach
³/₄ pound skinless, boneless chicken breasts
4 ounces thin spinach egg noodles
1¹/₂ teaspoons bottled chopped garlic in oil
Salt and freshly ground pepper

1. In a large saucepan or soup pot, combine the broth and 2 cups water. Add the spinach and bring to a boil, stirring to break up the spinach.

2. Meanwhile, cut the chicken into ³/₄-inch cubes. When the liquid boils, add the chicken and noodles. Cover, reduce the heat to medium-low and cook until the chicken is white but still moist in the center and the noodles are tender, 5 to 7 minutes.

3. Stir in the garlic in oil and season to taste with salt and pepper.

3 TO 4 SERVINGS

SPRING CHICKEN SOUP WITH ASPARAGUS AND EGG NOODLES

By leaving the tender tips in large pieces and cutting the tougher stalks into thinner slices, all the asparagus cooks evenly in the same amount of time.

$^3/_4$ pound skinless, boneless chicken breasts
$^3/_4$ pound slender asparagus
  8 cups chicken broth
1$^3/_4$ cups fine egg noodles (5 ounces)
  8 green onions
    Salt and freshly ground pepper

1. Cut the chicken into $^1/_2$-inch cubes. Cut the asparagus tips into 1-inch lengths and thinly slice the stalks.

2. In a large saucepan or soup pot, bring the chicken broth to a boil over high heat. Add the chicken, asparagus and egg noodles. Return to a boil, reduce the heat to medium-low and cook, partly covered, until the noodles are tender and the chicken is white but still moist in the center, 5 to 7 minutes.

3. While the soup is cooking, thinly slice the green onions. Stir the green onions into the soup and season with salt and pepper to taste before serving.

4 TO 6 SERVINGS

TARRAGON CHICKEN AND RICE SOUP

This fragrant soup makes a lovely light lunch or substantial first course. Serve with seeded bread sticks.

8 cups chicken broth
³/₄ pound skinless, boneless chicken breasts
8 green onions
1¹/₂ cups quick-cooking rice
1¹/₂ teaspoons dried tarragon
   Salt and freshly ground pepper

1. In a large saucepan or soup pot, bring the chicken broth to a boil. Meanwhile, cut the chicken into ¹/₂-inch cubes. Thinly slice the green onions.

2. Add the chicken to the broth and reduce the heat to medium-low. Cover and cook for 2 minutes.

3. Stir in the rice and tarragon and cook, covered, over medium-low heat until the rice is tender and the chicken is white but still moist in the center, about 6 minutes.

4. Stir the sliced green onions into the soup. Season with salt and pepper to taste.

4 TO 6 SERVINGS

TORTELLINI GARLIC-CHICKEN SOUP

Frozen cheese tortellini are one of our favorite quick-cooking products. They're used here in a chicken soup made bright with peas and flavorful with another good addition to the larder— chopped garlic in oil—to make a terrific meal.

> 6 cups chicken broth
> 1/2 pound skinless, boneless chicken breasts
> 1 pound frozen cheese tortellini
> 2 cups frozen peas, preferably tiny peas
> 1 1/2 teaspoons bottled chopped garlic in oil
> Salt and freshly ground pepper

1. In a large saucepan or soup pot, combine the chicken broth and 2 cups water. Cover and bring to a boil.

2. Meanwhile, cut the chicken into thin strips. When the liquid boils, add the chicken, tortellini and peas. Cover, reduce the heat to medium-low and cook until the tortellini are tender, 6 to 8 minutes.

3. Stir in the garlic in oil and season to taste with salt and pepper.

4 TO 6 SERVINGS

CHICKEN TORTILLA SOUP

Monterey Jack cheese studded with the pleasantly hot bite of jalapeño peppers is now sold pretty much everywhere. With its combination of flavors, it's the perfect final addition to spark this savory soup. If you want even more flavor, you could use a spicy type of tortilla chip.

1¼ pounds skinless, boneless chicken breasts
4 teaspoons chili powder
12 ounces Monterey Jack cheese with jalapeños
1 bag (9 ounces) tortilla chips
2 cans (14 to 16 ounces) Southwestern-style stewed tomatoes

1. Cut the chicken into 1-inch cubes and toss with the chili powder to season all over. Shred the cheese in a food processor or on the large holes of a hand grater. Break the tortilla chips into bite-size pieces and set aside.

2. In a large saucepan or soup pot, combine the tomatoes and their juices with 4 cups water. Bring to a boil. Add the chicken, reduce the heat to medium-low and simmer until the chicken is white but still moist in the center, 7 to 8 minutes.

3. Divide half the tortilla chips and shredded cheese among 6 soup bowls. Ladle the soup into the bowls. Pass the remaining cheese and broken tortilla chips on the side.

6 SERVINGS

CHICKEN-VEGETABLE
ALPHABET SOUP

Alphabet-shaped noodles delight young and old alike in this hearty vegetable soup. Add a salad and some cornbread for a really good meal.

1 can (14 to 16 ounces) Italian-style stewed tomatoes
1 package (1 pound) frozen mixed vegetables
3/4 pound skinless, boneless chicken breasts
1/3 cup (2 ounces) alphabet noodles
2 teaspoons mixed Italian seasoning
   Salt and freshly ground pepper

1. In a large saucepan or soup pot, combine the stewed tomatoes, 4 cups water and the frozen vegetables. Cover and bring to a boil over high heat.

2. Meanwhile, cut the chicken into thin slices or 1/2-inch chunks. Add to the pot along with the alphabet noodles and Italian seasoning. Cover and cook over medium-low heat until the pasta is tender and the chicken is white but still moist in the center, 6 to 8 minutes. Season with salt and pepper to taste.

3 TO 4 SERVINGS

CHICKEN AND WHITE BEAN SOUP WITH PESTO

Of the "international" mixtures of frozen vegetables, we have found that the Italian combination—broccoli, beans, tomato, zucchini and onion—is one of the best and most consistent around the country. It's terrific in this wonderful supper soup, which gets a real boost of flavor from good-quality purchased pesto sauce.

6 cups chicken broth
1 package (1 pound) frozen mixed Italian vegetables
3/4 pound skinless, boneless chicken breasts
1 can (1 pound) white beans (cannellini)
1/3 cup purchased pesto sauce

1. Combine the broth and the vegetables in a large saucepan or soup pot, cover and bring to a boil over high heat.

2. Cut the chicken into 1/2-inch strips and add to the soup. Simmer, partially covered, over medium-low heat for 5 minutes. Drain the beans, add to the soup and simmer for 2 minutes longer.

3. Ladle the soup into bowls and top each serving with a spoonful of pesto sauce.

4 TO 5 SERVINGS

CREAM OF CHICKEN SOUP WITH ZUCCHINI AND SAFFRON

Saffron lends its brilliant orange-yellow color and distinctively pungent flavor to this delicate cream soup. Add a baguette of French bread and a salad of sliced beets and endive for a spectacular light meal.

3/4 pound skinless, boneless chicken breasts
1 small zucchini
3 cups chicken broth
2 cups heavy cream
1/2 teaspoon crushed saffron threads
   Salt and freshly ground black pepper

1. Cut the chicken into 1/2-inch cubes. In a food processor or on the large holes of a hand grater, shred the zucchini.

2. Combine the chicken broth, cream and saffron in a large saucepan or soup pot and bring to a boil. Add the chicken and zucchini, partly cover and reduce the heat to medium-low. Simmer until the chicken is white in the center, about 5 minutes.

3. Season with salt and pepper to taste and serve.

3 TO 4 SERVINGS

2 STEWS AND CASSEROLES

Liberation is the word that comes immediately to mind when thinking about present-day chicken stews and casseroles—freedom from the tyranny of long simmering. Before ready availability of the skinless and boneless chicken breast, stewing or braising chicken (that is, cooking it in a large or small amount of liquid) was a several-hour-long task, whether you used a tough old fowl (which, though admittedly full of flavor, requires many hours to tenderize) or simply cut-up chicken parts. So we now turn happily to chicken breasts for these warm, satisfying dishes, aided and abetted by several new convenience products.

But first we must start with the right cooking vessel. In the old days, bulky chicken parts or whole chickens necessitated using a big pot. These days we much prefer our trusty large heavy frying pan, which has a good lid. Pre-browning is easier, and liquids come to a boil and reduce faster in that wide, shallow pan. A wide flameproof casserole, of enameled cast-iron, also works well.

Frozen vegetables are appearing in lots of inventive and interesting combinations, and we have put this quality "convenience food" to excellent use in many of these stews and casseroles. We've also found that quick-cooking rice (both white and brown) is much improved, a terrific addition to the staples on the quick cook's pantry shelf.

BASQUE-STYLE CHICKEN AND RICE WITH OLIVES

Pimiento-stuffed olives add their pleasantly salty tang to this dish inspired by the Basque cooking of the Pyrenees mountains of Spain. Add a salad of greens simply dressed with olive oil and balsamic vinegar, a loaf of crusty bread and a glass of red wine for a truly fine meal.

1 pound skinless, boneless chicken breasts
  Salt and freshly ground pepper
3 garlic cloves
3 tablespoons olive oil
2 cups quick-cooking rice
1 cup pimiento-stuffed green olives

1. Cut the chicken into strips about ½ inch wide. Season very lightly with salt and generously with pepper. Finely chop the garlic.

2. Heat the oil in a large frying pan. Add the chicken and cook over medium-high heat until the chicken is browned and white but still moist in the center, about 1½ minutes per side. Add the garlic to the pan and cook until soft and fragrant, 30 to 60 seconds.

3. Add 2 cups water and the rice to the pan with the chicken. Bring to a simmer, cover and let stand off heat for 5 minutes, until the rice is tender and the water is absorbed.

4. While the dish is standing, slice the olives. Just before serving, stir them into the rice and chicken with a fork, fluffing the rice.

4 SERVINGS

BISTRO-STYLE CHICKEN WITH TOMATOES AND ROSEMARY

4 skinless, boneless chicken breast halves
(about 5 ounces each)
Salt and freshly ground pepper
3 garlic cloves
3 tablespoons olive oil
1½ teaspoons dried rosemary
1 can (14 to 16 ounces) Italian-style stewed tomatoes

1. Pound the chicken breasts slightly to flatten evenly and season with salt and pepper. Finely chop the garlic.

2. Heat the oil in a large frying pan. Add the chicken breasts and cook over medium-high heat, turning once, until browned, about 2 minutes per side.

3. Reduce the heat to medium-low. Add the garlic and rosemary and cook, stirring, until the garlic is softened and fragrant, about 1 minute.

4. Stir in the tomatoes and their juice along with ¼ cup water. Bring to a boil over high heat, reduce the heat to medium, cover and cook, until the chicken is white throughout but still moist, 3 to 4 minutes. If the sauce is a little too liquid, remove the chicken breasts to a platter and boil the sauce over high heat until reduced and thickened, about 1 minute. Season with salt and pepper to taste, pour the sauce over the chicken and serve.

4 SERVINGS

BRUNSWICK STEW

Our shortened version of Brunswick stew calls for frozen mixed vegetables, which usually include beans, peas, corn, carrots and sometimes lima beans. Try to find a mixture that does have the limas, because they're very much an integral part of the classic stew. Buttermilk biscuits and a salad of winter greens would be perfect accompaniments.

1 package (10 ounces) frozen mixed vegetables
1 pound skinless, boneless chicken breasts
  Salt and freshly ground pepper
1 teaspoon dried thyme leaves
4 tablespoons butter
1 can (14 to 16 ounces) stewed tomatoes and juice

1. Thaw the frozen vegetables in a microwave oven on High for 1 minute or place in a colander and rinse with warm water.

2. Cut the chicken breasts into 1-inch chunks. Season with about $1/4$ teaspoon each salt and pepper and with the thyme. Heat the butter in a large frying pan. Add the chicken and cook over medium heat, stirring occasionally, until lightly browned, about 2 minutes.

3. Add the tomatoes with their juice and the vegetables to the frying pan. Simmer, uncovered, until the chicken is white but still moist in the center and the vegetables are tender, about 3 minutes longer.

4 SERVINGS

CHICKEN CACCIATORE

Fettuccine tossed with scallions and Parmesan, and a green vegetable such as broccoli, make terrific accompaniments to this hearty autumn Italian chicken stew.

1 pound skinless, boneless chicken breasts
  Salt and freshly ground pepper
8 ounces fresh mushrooms
2 garlic cloves
4 tablespoons olive oil
1 can (14 to 16 ounces) Italian-style stewed tomatoes

1. Cut each piece of chicken crosswise in half and season with salt and pepper. Slice or quarter the mushrooms. Chop the garlic.

2. Heat 2½ tablespoons of the oil in a large frying pan. Add the chicken and cook over medium-high heat, turning, until lightly browned, about 1½ minutes per side. Remove to a plate, leaving the drippings in the pan.

3. Heat the remaining 1½ tablespoons of oil in the pan. Add the mushrooms and cook over medium-high heat, stirring, until they are lightly browned, about 2 minutes. Add the garlic and cook, stirring, for 1 minute.

4. Stir in the tomatoes and their juice, return the chicken and any juices that have accumulated on the plate to the pan, cover and simmer over low heat until the chicken is white throughout but still moist, about 4 minutes. Season with salt and pepper to taste.

4 SERVINGS

CHINESE POACHED CHICKEN

Simple, light and flavorful, this delicately poached chicken is best with steamed white or brown rice or Oriental noodles and a salad of grated or julienned carrots and sweet peppers.

> 1 pound skinless, boneless chicken breasts
> Freshly ground pepper
> 8 green onions
> 1¼ cups chicken broth
> 3 tablespoons pale dry sherry
> 2 tablespoons minced fresh ginger
> Salt

1. Cut the chicken breasts into 2½-inch pieces and season with pepper. Cut the green onions, including the green tops, into thin diagonal slices.

2. Place the chicken in a frying pan or shallow saucepan. Add the broth, sherry and ginger. Bring to a simmer over high heat. Cover, reduce the heat to medium-low and cook for 3 minutes.

3. Uncover and simmer until the chicken is white throughout but still juicy, 3 to 5 minutes longer. Stir in the sliced green onions and season with salt and pepper to taste.

4. Serve in soup plates, with some of the poaching liquid and green onions spooned over each portion of chicken.

4 SERVINGS

COQ AU VIN

This quickened and streamlined version of *coq au vin* is great for a group dinner on a cold winter evening. Serve it with boiled new potatoes in their jackets, sautéed mushrooms and a green salad.

6 ounces (8 or 9 slices) thinly sliced bacon
1½ pounds skinless, boneless chicken breasts
    Freshly ground pepper
2 cups frozen pearl onions
1½ teaspoons dried thyme
1½ cups dry red wine

1. Cut the bacon into ½-inch pieces. Cut the chicken into 1½-inch cubes and season generously with pepper.

2. Cook the bacon in a large frying pan over medium-high heat, stirring frequently, until it begins to brown and renders its fat, about 2 minutes. Add the chicken pieces and cook, stirring, until lightly browned, about 2 minutes.

3. Add the pearl onions, thyme and wine to the pan. Bring to a boil, cover and reduce the heat to medium. Cover and cook for 3 minutes. Uncover the pan and cook until the sauce is slightly reduced and the chicken is white but still moist in the center, 2 to 3 minutes longer. Season with additional salt and pepper to taste.

4 TO 6 SERVINGS

COUNTRY CAPTAIN CHICKEN

This curried chicken dish probably originated in Savannah, Georgia, which was a major shipping port for the spice trade in the last century. Serve it with plain white rice and steamed green beans. If you like, offer some chutney at the table as a condiment.

1 pound skinless, boneless chicken breasts
1 1/2 teaspoons curry powder
2 1/2 tablespoons vegetable oil
1 can (14 to 16 ounces) stewed tomatoes, with juice
1/2 cup raisins
1/2 teaspoon salt
1/4 teaspoon freshly ground pepper

1. Cut each piece of chicken crosswise in half. Sprinkle the curry powder over both sides. Heat the oil in a large frying pan. Add the chicken and cook over medium heat, turning once, until lightly browned, about 2 minutes per side.

2. Add the stewed tomatoes, raisins, salt, pepper and 1/3 cup of water. Cover the pan, reduce the heat to medium-low and cook until the chicken is white throughout, 3 to 5 minutes.

3. Remove the chicken to a serving dish. Boil the sauce until slightly reduced, 1 to 2 minutes. Pour over the chicken and serve.

4 SERVINGS

CUMIN-BRAISED ARIZONA CHICKEN

For extra flavor, toast whole cumin seeds lightly and grind in a
spice grinder or mini food processor. This flavorful Southwestern
stew would be nice with a corn and black bean salad and warm
flour tortillas.

    1 pound skinless, boneless chicken breasts
      Salt and freshly ground pepper
1 1/2 teaspoons ground cumin
    2 tablespoons vegetable oil
    1 can (14 to 16 ounces) Southwestern-style stewed tomatoes
    1 can (11 ounces) corn niblets

1. Cut the chicken into 1 1/2-inch cubes and season lightly with salt
and pepper. Sprinkle with the cumin, rubbing it in evenly.

2. Heat the oil in a large frying pan. Add the chicken and cook
over medium-high heat, turning, until lightly browned, about
1 1/2 minutes per side.

3. Add the stewed tomatoes with their juice. Drain the corn and
add it to the pan. Cover, reduce the heat to medium-low and
simmer for 5 minutes. Season with salt and pepper to taste before
serving.

4 SERVINGS

CHICKEN BRAISED WITH FENNEL AND TOMATOES

If you love the licorice flavor of fennel, this dish, which is also enhanced with fennel seed, is definitely for you. As side dishes, we suggest creamy polenta and a salad of radicchio and endive.

1 pound skinless, boneless chicken breasts
  Salt and freshly ground pepper
1 small fennel bulb (8 ounces)
3 tablespoons extra virgin olive oil
1 can (14 to 16 ounces) Italian-style stewed tomatoes
1 teaspoon fennel seed

1. Cut the chicken into $2^1/_2$-inch pieces and season with salt and pepper. Cut the fennel crosswise into thin slices.

2. Heat 2 tablespoons of the olive oil in a large frying pan. Add the chicken and cook over medium-high heat until browned, about $1^1/_2$ minutes per side. Remove to a plate, leaving the drippings in the pan.

3. Add the fennel to the pan along with the remaining 1 tablespoon oil and cook, stirring, until lightly browned, 2 to 3 minutes.

4. Add the tomatoes to the pan along with $1/_4$ cup water and the fennel seed. Bring to a boil, then reduce the heat to medium-low. Return the chicken and any accumulated juices on the plate to the pan. Cover and cook until the chicken is white but still moist, about 5 minutes.

4 SERVINGS

LATIN AMERICAN
CHICKEN AND RICE

8 ounces chorizo, kielbasa or hot Italian sausage
1 pound skinless, boneless chicken breasts
2 cups quick-cooking rice
1 can (14 to 16 ounces) Southwestern-style stewed tomatoes
1/2 pound medium shelled and deveined shrimp
1/2 teaspoon salt
1/4 teaspoon freshly ground black pepper

1. Cut the chorizo into slices about 1/4 inch thick. Cut the chicken crosswise into strips about 1/2 inch wide.

2. In a large frying pan, cook the chorizo over medium-high heat, stirring, for 2 minutes. Add the chicken strips and continue to cook, stirring, until the chicken and sausage are browned, about 2 minutes longer. Use a slotted spoon to remove the meats to a plate, leaving the drippings in the pan.

3. Add 2 cups water to the pan along with the rice, tomatoes and their juice, shrimp, salt and pepper. Bring to a boil over high heat, stirring up the browned bits in the bottom of the pan. Reduce the heat to medium-low and distribute the sausage and chicken over the tomato-rice mixture. Cover and cook until the chicken and shrimp are cooked through and the rice is tender, about 5 minutes.

6 TO 8 SERVINGS

CHICKEN AND LEEK FRICASSEE

Though the dictionary is somewhat vague on the difference between a fricassee and a stew, this delicate dish tastes great no matter how you define it. Buttered green noodles and steamed whole baby carrots would add lovely color to the plate.

3 medium leeks
1 pound skinless, boneless chicken breasts
    Salt and freshly ground pepper
3 tablespoons butter
$1/2$ cup dry white wine
$1/2$ cup heavy cream

1. Trim the leeks so that you are using the white and pale green parts only. Halve the leeks lengthwise and rinse very well to remove any grit. Cut crosswise into thin slices. Cut the chicken breasts into strips about 1 inch wide and season with salt and pepper.

2. Heat the butter in a large frying pan over medium heat. Add the chicken and turn to coat with the butter. Add the leeks and $1/4$ cup of water. Reduce the heat to medium-low, cover and cook for 5 minutes.

3. Add the wine and cream. Bring to a boil, reduce the heat and simmer, uncovered, until the sauce is slightly reduced and the chicken is white but still moist in the center, 2 to 3 minutes. Season the sauce with salt and pepper to taste.

4 SERVINGS

MOROCCAN CHICKEN WITH APRICOTS AND COUSCOUS

Heady with the fragrance of curry powder and the sweetness of dried apricots, this chicken couscous dish makes great party fare for six people, and could easily be multiplied for a larger group.

1½ pounds skinless, boneless chicken breasts
4 teaspoons curry powder
¼ cup vegetable oil
1½ cups dried apricots (about 6 ounces)
¾ teaspoon salt
¼ teaspoon freshly ground pepper
1½ cups instant couscous

1. Cut the chicken breasts into ¾-inch-wide strips and season on all sides with the curry powder. Heat the oil in a large frying pan. Add the chicken and cook over medium-high heat for about 2 minutes per side, until browned outside and white in the center. Remove the chicken to a plate, leaving the drippings in the pan.

2. Cut the apricots into ¼-inch slivers and add them to the pan along with 3 cups water and the salt, pepper and couscous. Arrange the chicken over the couscous, bring to a boil and simmer for 1 minute.

3. Cover the pan, remove from the heat and let stand for 5 minutes, until the couscous has absorbed the liquid. Fluff with a fork and serve.

6 SERVINGS

PESTO RISOTTO

This isn't really an authentic risotto, but with jarred pesto sauces available in the supermarket, its quick preparation and great taste make it a wonderful main course that is almost a meal in itself.

1¼ pounds skinless, boneless chicken breasts
2 red bell peppers
1 medium yellow crookneck squash
¼ teaspoon salt
¼ teaspoon freshly ground pepper
2½ cups quick-cooking white rice
⅔ cup pesto sauce

1. Cut the chicken into ¾-inch pieces. Cut the peppers into ½-inch dice. Cut the squash lengthwise, then slice crosswise.

2. Place the chicken in a heavy 3-quart saucepan; add the bell peppers, salt, pepper and 3 cups water. Heat over high heat. Just before the water comes to a boil, add the squash. Bring to a boil, then stir in the rice and pesto. Cover the pot and remove from the heat.

3. Let stand, covered, for 5 minutes, until the liquid is absorbed and the rice is tender. Season with additional salt and pepper to taste.

6 TO 8 SERVINGS

QUICK CHICKEN AND DUMPLINGS

Tubes of biscuit dough, usually found in the dairy section of the supermarket, are a terrific boon to busy cooks short of time. Here, the rounds of biscuit dough steam over a simmering stew to make perfect, puffy dumplings. Serve the stew with a big salad of greens sprinkled with cubes of crisply cooked bacon.

3 cups chicken broth
1 package (1 pound) frozen mixed stew vegetables
1 pound skinless, boneless chicken breasts
1½ teaspoons poultry seasoning
¼ teaspoon freshly ground pepper
1 tube (10 ounces) refrigerated biscuit dough

1. In a large frying pan, combine the chicken broth and vegetables. Bring to a boil over high heat. Meanwhile, cut the chicken into 1-inch chunks, season with the poultry seasoning and pepper and add to the broth and vegetables.

2. Peel off 8 rounds of biscuit dough and place them on top of the simmering stew, trying to allow about ½ inch between each biscuit. Reduce the heat to medium-low, cover and cook for 10 minutes. The dumplings will have risen as they steam and should be cooked through.

3. Serve the chicken stew in shallow bowls with the dumplings on top.

4 SERVINGS

Chicken and Sausage Jambalaya

8 ounces smoked garlic sausage, such as kielbasa or
   andouille
1 pound skinless, boneless chicken breasts
1 large green bell pepper
1½ cups quick-cooking rice
1 can (14 to 16 ounces) stewed tomatoes
½ teaspoon salt
¼ teaspoon freshly ground pepper

1. Cut the sausage into slices about ¼ inch thick and cut the
chicken into 2-inch pieces. Core and seed the green pepper and cut
into 1-inch squares.

2. Cook the sausage in a large frying pan over medium-high heat,
stirring often, until browned, about 2 minutes. Add the chicken
and the green pepper and cook, stirring often, until the chicken is
browned on both sides, about 2 minutes longer. Use a slotted
spoon to remove the meats and pepper to a plate, leaving the
drippings in the pan.

3. Add 1½ cups water, the rice, tomatoes with their juice, salt and
pepper to the pan. Bring to a simmer. Distribute the sausage,
chicken and peppers over the tomato-rice mixture. Cover and cook
over low heat until the chicken is white but still moist in the center
and the rice is tender, about 5 minutes.

4 to 5 servings

SESAME CHICKEN AND BROWN RICE

Quick-cooking brown rice is a real boon because although many of us love brown rice, it takes about 45 minutes to cook the standard variety. We think this is every bit as good.

$1/2$ teaspoon salt
2 cups quick-cooking brown rice
1 pound skinless, boneless chicken breasts
   Freshly ground pepper
6 green onions
3 tablespoons Asian sesame oil
2 tablespoons soy sauce

1. In a small saucepan, bring 2 cups of water to a boil. Add the salt and the rice, cover and cook over low heat for 5 minutes. Remove from the heat and let stand for 5 minutes longer, until the rice is tender.

2. Meanwhile, cut the chicken into strips about $1/2$ inch wide and season with the pepper. Thinly slice the green onions.

3. Heat the sesame oil in a large frying pan. Add the chicken strips and cook over medium heat, stirring, until cooked through, about 3 minutes. Add $1/4$ cup water to the chicken and simmer, uncovered, stirring up any browned bits that cling to the pan, for 1 minute. Add the soy sauce, stir in the cooked brown rice and sprinkle the green onion slices on top.

4 SERVINGS

SPICY CHICKEN CHILI

If you're having a group of people for supper, what could be nicer than a big pot of chili? Serve this hot and spicy dish with plain boiled rice or squares of hot cornbread. A refreshing salad of grapefruit and avocado would make a lovely accompaniment.

1½ pounds skinless, boneless chicken breasts
  3 tablespoons vegetable oil
  2 tablespoons chili powder, or to taste
  2 cans (14 to 16 ounces) kidney beans
  2 cans (14 to 16 ounces) Southwestern-style stewed tomatoes
  ½ teaspoon salt
  ½ teaspoon pepper

1. Cut the chicken into 1-inch pieces and pulse in a food processor until coarsely ground. Do not grind to a paste.

2. Heat the oil in a large saucepan or flameproof casserole. Add the chicken and the chili powder. Cook over medium heat, stirring, until the chicken has lost its raw look, about 2 minutes.

3. Drain the kidney beans and add them to the pot along with the tomatoes with their juice, salt, pepper and 1½ cups water. Cover and bring to a boil over high heat. Reduce the heat to medium-low and simmer, uncovered, for 6 to 8 minutes, mashing some of the beans against the side of the pot to thicken the chili a bit. Season with additional salt and pepper to taste before serving.

6 TO 8 SERVINGS

BRAISED SPRINGTIME CHICKEN WITH PEAS AND TARRAGON

The frozen vegetable combination of green peas and small pearl onions is especially well suited to this lovely, delicate springtime dish. Add some crusty French bread and a salad of sliced radishes and lettuce for a delicious seasonal supper.

1 pound skinless, boneless chicken breasts
    Salt and freshly ground pepper
3 tablespoons butter
2 cups frozen peas and pearl onions
1 cup heavy cream
1 teaspoon dried tarragon

1. Cut the chicken breasts into 1½-inch cubes and season with salt and pepper. Heat the butter in a large frying pan. Add the chicken and cook over medium heat, stirring several times, until pale golden, about 4 minutes.

2. Add the peas and pearl onions and ⅓ cup water. Cover and simmer over medium heat for 3 minutes. Add the cream and the tarragon. Cook, uncovered, over medium heat for about 2 minutes, until the chicken is cooked through; the sauce will remain quite soupy. Season with salt and pepper to taste before serving.

4 SERVINGS

SOUTHWESTERN POACHED CHICKEN WITH GREEN CHILES

Cumin and cilantro add their distinctively earthy flavors to this lightly poached chicken. Ladle the chicken and its flavorful poaching liquid over rice, if you like, and serve a green salad with avocado on the side.

   1 pound skinless, boneless chicken breasts
1 1/2 teaspoons ground cumin
  1/2 teaspoon freshly ground pepper
1 1/4 cups chicken broth
   1 can (4 ounces) chopped green chiles
  1/4 cup chopped cilantro
    Salt and freshly ground pepper

1. Cut the chicken into 1 1/2-inch strips and season all over with the cumin and pepper. Place in a medium frying pan or large saucepan and add the broth. Bring to a simmer, cover and cook over medium-low heat for 3 minutes.

2. Uncover, add the green chiles and simmer over medium heat until the chicken is white but still moist in the center, about 2 minutes.

3. Stir in the cilantro and season with salt and pepper to taste. Serve the chicken in soup plates, with some of the poaching liquid and chiles spooned over each portion.

4 SERVINGS

3 Sautés and
Skillet Dishes

Skinless, boneless chicken breasts and their cousins—thinly sliced chicken cutlets—are ideally suited to sautéing. Four of the breast halves fit neatly into a large skillet, and when a few (namely four!) more ingredients are added to make a lively pan sauce, you've got a really wonderful centerpiece to a truly good meal.

To sauté thinly sliced chicken cutlets, you'll need a large (10- to 12-inch) heavy frying pan with a tight lid. If you don't already own one, it's well worth the investment. You'll probably find that you will use it to cook so many things, including chicken stews and stir-fries as well, that you'll bless the day you brought it home.

When a recipe calls for chicken breasts to be "pounded lightly," simply use the heel of your hand to flatten the breast to a more or less even thickness; or place the meat under a piece of plastic wrap and use a mallet, a rolling pin or the bottom of a heavy, small pot to exert more weight. A slightly flattened piece of chicken will cook more evenly, reducing the risk of overcooking part of the meat before the thicker part is cooked through.

If a recipe calls for thinly sliced cutlets, we assume they are from skinless, boneless breasts. You can either buy chicken breasts and slice them horizontally yourself into thin *paillards,* or cutlets, or look for them sliced in your meat case. Slicing usually adds something to the cost per pound, so as always, weigh the cost versus the convenience of the product.

CHICKEN ALMONDINE

The richness of toasted almonds in this sauce makes a lovely counterpoint to the chicken. Parslied new potatoes and steamed zucchini will round out this meal beautifully.

1 pound thinly sliced chicken cutlets
  Salt and freshly ground pepper
6 green onions
4 tablespoons butter
1/2 cup sliced almonds
1 cup dry white wine

1. Season the chicken cutlets with salt and pepper. Thinly slice the green onions. Heat 3 tablespoons of the butter in a large frying pan. Add the chicken and cook over medium heat, turning once, until golden brown and cooked through, about 2 minutes per side. Remove to a plate, leaving the drippings in the pan.

2. Reduce the heat to medium-low and add the remaining 1 tablespoon of butter and the sliced almonds to the pan. Cook, stirring frequently, until the nuts are just beginning to color, about 2 minutes.

3. Add the sliced green onions to the pan and cook, stirring, until they are softened and the nuts are lightly browned, about 1 minute. Add the wine and boil, uncovered, until the sauce is slightly reduced, 1 to 2 minutes. Return the chicken and any accumulated juices to the pan, heat through and serve.

4 SERVINGS

CHICKEN WITH
APPLE-CORNBREAD STUFFING

Packaged cornbread stuffing mix and sautéed tart apple make a wonderful topping for this quick skillet dish. For a golden brown finish, run the cooked dish under a hot broiler for a minute or so. If you do so, be sure your skillet handle is flameproof.

    1 pound thinly sliced chicken cutlets
      Freshly ground pepper
    1 small tart apple, such as Granny Smith
    4 tablespoons butter
    1½ cups dry packaged cornbread stuffing mix
    1 cup chicken broth

1. Season the chicken cutlets with pepper. Peel and core the apple and cut it into ½-inch dice.

2. Heat 3 tablespoons of the butter in a large frying pan. Add the chicken and cook over medium heat until lightly browned and cooked through, about 2 minutes per side. With tongs, remove the chicken to a serving platter, leaving the drippings in the pan.

3. Melt the remaining 1 tablespoon of butter in the frying pan. Add the diced apple and cook over medium heat, stirring frequently, for 2 minutes. Add the stuffing mix and broth and reduce the heat to medium-low. Cook, stirring, until the liquid is absorbed but the stuffing is still moist, about 2 minutes.

4. Spoon the stuffing over the chicken breasts and serve at once.

4 SERVINGS

AUTUMN CHICKEN SAUTÉ WITH DRIED FRUITS

Dried packaged mixed fruits, which usually consist of apples, pears, apricots and prunes, form the basis for this very tasty sauce. Wild rice and a salad of mixed greens would be nice accompaniments.

1⅓ cups (7 ounces) mixed dried fruits
  6 skinless, boneless chicken breast halves
    (about 5 ounces each)
    Salt and freshly ground pepper
  4 tablespoons butter
⅓ cup chopped shallots
  3 tablespoons apple or apricot brandy

1. In a small bowl, pour 1½ cups boiling water over the mixed fruits and set aside to steep.

2. Pound the chicken breasts slightly to flatten evenly; season with salt and pepper. Heat the butter in a large frying pan. Add the chicken breasts and cook over medium heat until nicely browned, about 2 minutes per side.

3. Add the shallots to the pan and cook, stirring, for 30 seconds. Add the soaked fruits and their liquid and cook, uncovered, over medium heat until the chicken is white in the center and the sauce is slightly reduced, 3 to 4 minutes. Add the brandy and cook for 1 minute longer. Season with salt and pepper to taste and serve.

6 SERVINGS

SAUTÉED CHICKEN WITH BANANAS AND RUM

Chili powder is the major seasoning in this Caribbean-style chicken dish. Since different brands vary in spiciness and saltiness, you might want to add a little more or less to taste.

1 pound thinly sliced chicken cutlets
2 teaspoons chili powder
1 large, slightly underripe banana
4 tablespoons butter
$1/2$ cup light rum
    Salt

1. Season both sides of the chicken cutlets with the chili powder. Peel and slice the banana.

2. Melt 3 tablespoons of the butter in a large frying pan over medium heat. Add the chicken and cook, turning once, until lightly browned outside and white in the center but still moist, about 2 minutes per side. Remove to a warm plate.

3. Melt the remaining 1 tablespoon of butter in the pan. Add the banana slices and cook over medium-low heat, stirring, until softened and lightly browned, about 1 minute.

4. Pour the rum and $1/2$ cup water over the bananas. Boil over medium-heat heat until slightly reduced and thickened, 1 to 2 minutes. Season the sauce with salt to taste. Pour the sauce and bananas over the chicken and serve.

4 SERVINGS

BATTER-FRIED CHICKEN FINGERS

Cole slaw and French fries would be terrific accompaniments to this "shallow-fried" chicken. A squirt of cider or malt vinegar is a nice condiment.

1½ pounds well-trimmed skinless, boneless chicken breasts
¾ cup flour
¾ teaspoon baking soda
¾ teaspoon salt
¾ teaspoon freshly ground pepper
1½ tablespoons cider vinegar
   Vegetable oil, for shallow frying

1. Cut the chicken breasts crosswise into ½-inch-wide strips. In a small bowl, whisk together the flour, baking soda, salt and pepper. In a measuring cup, mix ¾ cup water with the vinegar. Whisk the liquid into the dry ingredients until smooth.

2. Pour the oil into a large, heavy frying pan (preferably cast-iron) to a depth of about ½ inch. Heat until a teaspoon of the batter sizzles when dropped into the oil (about 360 degrees F.).

3. Dip the chicken strips into the batter, allowing the excess to drip back into the bowl. In 2 batches, fry the chicken until rich golden brown on one side, about 2 minutes. Using tongs, turn the fingers to the other side and fry about 2 minutes longer, until golden brown on the second side and white throughout. Remove with tongs to a plate lined with paper towels and blot off any excess oil. Serve immediately.

4 TO 5 SERVINGS

SAUTÉED CHICKEN WITH BLUEBERRY VINEGAR SAUCE

Sweet fresh—or frozen—blueberries in combination with a splash of tart berry vinegar makes a delicious, summery chicken dish.

1 pound thinly sliced chicken cutlets
   Salt and freshly ground pepper
4 tablespoons butter
¼ cup minced shallots
1½ cups blueberries
3 tablespoons berry vinegar

1. Season the chicken cutlets with salt and pepper. Heat 3 tablespoons of the butter in a large nonreactive frying pan. Add the chicken and cook over medium heat, turning once, until golden brown and cooked through, about 2 minutes per side. Remove to a plate, leaving the drippings in the pan.

2. Melt the remaining 1 tablespoon of butter in the pan. Add the shallots and cook over medium heat, stirring, for 1 minute. Add the blueberries and ½ cup water. Boil over medium-high heat for 2 minutes. Using the back of a spoon, mash about one-quarter of the blueberries into the sauce to thicken it.

3. Stir in the vinegar and reduce the heat to medium-low. Return the chicken and any accumulated juices on the plate to the pan, simmer 1 minute to heat through and serve.

4 SERVINGS

CHICKEN WITH BOURBON-ORANGE SAUCE

1 pound thinly sliced chicken cutlets
Salt and freshly ground pepper
1 medium onion
2 medium oranges
4 tablespoons butter
¼ cup bourbon whiskey

1. Season the chicken cutlets with salt and pepper. Chop the onion. Grate 2 teaspoons of the colored zest and squeeze ⅓ cup of juice from 1½ oranges. Cut 4 thin slices from the remaining orange half, cut the slices in half and set aside.

2. Heat 3 tablespoons of the butter in a large frying pan. Add the chicken and cook over medium heat, turning once, until lightly browned and cooked through, about 2 minutes per side. Remove to a plate, leaving the drippings in the pan.

3. Melt the remaining 1 tablespoon of butter in the pan. Add the chopped onion and cook over medium heat for 2 minutes. Add the orange zest, orange juice, ½ cup water and the bourbon. Bring to a boil over medium-high heat and boil until the sauce is slightly reduced and thickened, 1 to 2 minutes.

4. Return the chicken and any accumulated juices to the sauce. Add the orange slices and simmer for 1 minute. Garnish each serving of chicken and sauce with a couple of orange slices.

4 SERVINGS

BRANDIED CHICKEN AU POIVRE

Serve this elegant dish with steamed asparagus, herbed rice pilaf and a leafy green salad to create a quick menu for entertaining.

4 skinless, boneless chicken breast halves
  (about 5 ounces each)
1/2 teaspoon salt
1 tablespoon coarsely ground pepper
3 tablespoons butter
1/4 cup Cognac or brandy
1 cup heavy cream

1. Pound the chicken breasts slightly to flatten evenly. Season with 1/4 teaspoon of the salt and sprinkle the pepper evenly over both sides. Melt the butter in a large frying pan over medium heat. Add the chicken and cook, turning once, until golden brown and almost white throughout, about 2½ minutes per side. Remove to a plate.

2. Pour the Cognac into the pan and boil, scraping up the browned bits on the bottom of the pan, until reduced by half, about 1 minute. Add the cream and bring to a boil over high heat. Boil until slightly reduced and thickened, 1 to 2 minutes. Season with salt and pepper to taste. Reduce the heat to medium.

3. Return the chicken to the pan, along with any juices that have accumulated on the plate. Simmer, turning the chicken over once, until heated though and white but still moist in the center, about 2 minutes.

4 SERVINGS

SAUTÉED CHICKEN WITH CAPERS AND LEMON BUTTER

Pickled capers add their distinctive salty tang to this lemony sauce. Orzo pilaf and sautéed zucchini are perfect accompaniments to this lovely (but quick) meal for two.

1/2 pound thinly sliced chicken cutlets
   Salt and freshly ground pepper
1 medium lemon
1 tablespoon butter
1 tablespoon olive oil
2 teaspoons drained tiny (nonpareil) capers

1. Season the chicken cutlets lightly with salt and generously with pepper. Grate 1/2 teaspoon of colored zest and squeeze 2 tablespoons of juice from the lemon.

2. Heat the butter and olive oil in a large frying pan. Add the chicken and cook over medium heat, turning once, until golden brown and cooked through, about 2 minutes per side. Remove to a serving plate, leaving the drippings in the pan.

3. Add 3 tablespoons water, the lemon juice, lemon zest and capers to the pan and cook, stirring up the browned bits from the bottom of the pan, for about 1 minute. Mash a few of the capers into the sauce with the back of a spoon. Pour the sauce over the chicken and serve.

2 SERVINGS

SAUTÉED CHICKEN WITH CARAWAY SEED AND ONIONS

This sauce is a pleasing interplay of flavors, with the rather exotic tang of the caraway seed to enliven things even more. Oven-roasted potatoes and whole green beans would round out the plate nicely.

4 skinless, boneless chicken breast halves
　　(about 5 ounces each)
　　Salt and freshly ground pepper
1 large onion
3 tablespoons butter
1 teaspoon caraway seed
1 cup dry white wine

1. Pound the chicken breasts slightly to flatten evenly. Season with salt and pepper. Thinly slice the onion.

2. Heat the butter in a large frying pan. Add the chicken breasts and cook over medium-high heat, turning once, until browned, about 2 minutes per side. Push the chicken to one side of the pan, add the onion and the caraway seed and stir to coat with butter. Cover and cook over medium heat until the onion is softened, 2 to 3 minutes.

3. Add the wine and cook over medium heat, uncovered, until the chicken is cooked through and the liquid is slightly reduced, 2 to 3 minutes longer. Season with salt and pepper to taste and serve.

4 SERVINGS

CARIBBEAN CUTLETS WITH PINEAPPLE AND JALAPEÑO PEPPERS

1 pound thinly sliced chicken cutlets
  Salt and freshly ground pepper
1 medium onion
2 to 3 pickled jalapeño peppers
4 tablespoons butter
1 can (8 ounces) pineapple chunks in light syrup

1. Season the chicken with salt and pepper. Chop the onion. Cut the jalapeños lengthwise in half and scrape out the seeds if desired. (Removing the seeds reduces the fire.) Mince the peppers.

2. Heat 3 tablespoons of the butter in a large frying pan. Add the chicken and cook over medium heat, turning once, until golden brown and cooked through, about 2 minutes per side. Remove to a plate, leaving the drippings in the pan.

3. Add the remaining 1 tablespoon of butter and the chopped onion to the pan. Cook over medium heat, stirring occasionally, until the onion is softened and lightly browned, about 4 minutes. Add the pineapple with its juice and ½ cup water to the pan. Simmer, uncovered, for 2 minutes.

4. Stir in the minced jalapeños. Season the sauce with salt and pepper to taste, spoon over the chicken and serve.

4 SERVINGS

CHICKEN WITH COUNTRY HAM AND RED-EYE GRAVY

This Southern specialty is great with squares of cornbread and cooked collard or turnip greens.

1 pound thinly sliced chicken cutlets
  Freshly ground pepper
2 ounces country ham or other smoked ham
3 tablespoons vegetable oil
1 teaspoon instant coffee powder
1 cup heavy cream
  Salt

1. Season the chicken cutlets generously with pepper. Cut the ham into ¼-inch dice; there should be about ½ cup.

2. Heat the oil in a large frying pan. Add the chicken and cook over medium-high heat, turning once, until browned and cooked through, about 1½ minutes per side. Remove to a serving plate, leaving the drippings in the pan.

3. Add the diced ham to the pan and cook over medium heat, stirring often, until tinged with brown, about 2 minutes.

4. Stir the instant coffee into the cream and add to the pan. Bring to a boil over high heat, scraping up any browned bits from the bottom of the pan. Boil, uncovered, until the sauce is slightly reduced and thickened, about 1 minute. Season with pepper and a little salt if necessary. Pour the sauce over the chicken and serve.

4 SERVINGS

CHICKEN WITH
CREAMY SORREL SAUCE

Sorrel, or sour grass, is a widely available green that has both a spring and a fall crop. Here it's cut into slivers (or *chiffonade*) and adds a distinctively delicious tang to this creamy sauce.

4 skinless, boneless chicken breast halves
   (about 5 ounces each)
$1/2$ teaspoon salt
$1/4$ teaspoon freshly ground pepper
1 small bunch of sorrel (about 3 ounces)
3 tablespoons butter
$1/4$ cup chopped shallots
1 cup heavy cream

1. Pound the chicken breasts slightly to flatten evenly and season with half of the salt and pepper. Roll the sorrel leaves into a cylinder and cut crosswise into thin slivers to make about 1 cup.

2. Heat the butter in a large frying pan. Add the chicken breasts and cook over medium-high heat, turning once, until pale golden brown, about 2 minutes per side.

3. Add the chopped shallots to the frying pan and cook, stirring, for 30 seconds. Stir in the sorrel, cream and remaining salt and pepper. Bring to a simmer, reduce the heat to medium-low and cook for 4 to 5 minutes, until the chicken is white but still moist in the center.

4 SERVINGS

FIVE-SPICE SHIITAKE CHICKEN SAUTÉ

An aromatic blend of ground cinnamon, cloves, Szechuan pepper, star anise and fennel, five-spice powder is one of China's wonderful contributions to our melting pot cuisine and is readily available in the Asian foods section of most supermarkets as well as in Chinese grocery stores.

1 pound thinly sliced chicken cutlets
2 teaspoons Chinese five-spice powder
³/₄ pound shiitake mushrooms
¹/₄ cup vegetable oil
2 tablespoons soy sauce

1. Sprinkle both sides of the chicken cutlets with the five-spice powder, rubbing it in well. Trim and slice the mushrooms.

2. Heat 3 tablespoons of the oil in a large frying pan. Add the chicken and cook over medium-high heat until browned and cooked through, about 1¹/₂ minutes per side. Remove to a plate, leaving the drippings in the pan.

3. Heat the remaining 1 tablespoon of oil in the pan. Add the mushrooms and cook over medium-high heat, stirring, until lightly browned and quite tender, about 3 minutes.

4. Add ²/₃ cup water and the soy sauce to the pan. Boil, uncovered, until the sauce is slightly reduced, 1 to 2 minutes. Return the chicken and any accumulated juices to the pan and heat through.

4 SERVINGS

CHICKEN FLORENTINE

Spinach flavored with fresh garlic and Parmesan cheese makes a gorgeous green bed for this simply sautéed chicken.

1 package (10 ounces) frozen spinach
2 garlic cloves
1 pound thinly sliced chicken cutlets
Salt and freshly ground pepper
1/4 cup olive oil
3 tablespoons grated Parmesan cheese

1. Thaw the spinach in a microwave on High for 1 to 2 minutes. Drain well. Squeeze to remove as much moisture as possible. Finely chop the garlic.

2. Season the chicken cutlets with salt and pepper. Heat 3 tablespoons of the oil in a large frying pan. Add the chicken and cook over medium-high heat, turning, until lightly browned and cooked throughout, 1 1/2 to 2 minutes per side. Remove to a plate and cover with foil to keep warm.

3. Add the remaining 1 tablespoon oil to the pan and reduce the heat to medium. Add the garlic and cook, stirring, until softened and fragrant, about 1 minute. Stir in the spinach and cook, stirring, until heated through, about 1 minute. Stir in the cheese and remove from the heat. Season with salt and pepper to taste.

4. To serve, spread the spinach on a platter and arrange the chicken on top. Drizzle any juices from the plate over all.

4 SERVINGS

GARLIC CHICKEN WITH BALSAMIC VINEGAR

This dish is for garlic lovers! Serve baked potatoes to sop up the delectably potent sauce and a pepper salad.

```
 1 pound thinly sliced chicken cutlets
   Salt and freshly ground pepper
 4 garlic cloves
¼ cup extra virgin olive oil
 2 tablespoons balsamic vinegar
 3 tablespoons chopped fresh parsley
```

1. Season the chicken cutlets with salt and pepper. Finely chop the garlic.

2. Heat 3 tablespoons of the oil in a large frying pan. Add the chicken and cook over medium-high heat, turning once, until browned, about 1½ minutes per side. Remove to a plate, leaving the drippings in the pan.

3. Add the remaining 1 tablespoon of oil to the pan along with the garlic. Cook over medium-low heat, stirring, until softened but not brown, about 1 minute. Add the vinegar and ½ cup water to the pan. Bring to a boil, stirring up any browned bits from the bottom of the pan. Boil 1 minute. Stir in the parsley.

4. Return the chicken and any accumulated juices on the plate to the pan and simmer for 1 minute to heat through.

4 SERVINGS

CHICKEN IN GARLIC GREEN SAUCE

Green salsa gets its beautiful color from tomatillos, which have a sweet, lemony flavor. Its heat (and its saltiness) varies from brand to brand, so use one that you know and like. Warm tortillas and an orange and red onion salad make excellent accompaniments.

    4 skinless, boneless chicken breast halves
      (about 5 ounces each)
      Freshly ground pepper
    2 garlic cloves
    3 tablespoons vegetable oil
    1 cup green salsa or taco sauce
 1/4 cup chopped cilantro

1. Pound the chicken breasts slightly to flatten evenly. Season the chicken with pepper. Finely chop the garlic.

2. Heat the oil in a large frying pan. Add the chicken and cook over medium heat until the chicken is browned and almost cooked through, about 3 minutes per side. Remove to a plate, leaving the drippings in the pan.

3. Add the garlic to the pan and cook over medium heat, stirring, until softened but not browned, about 1 minute. Add the salsa along with 1/2 cup water. Bring to a simmer. Return the chicken and any accumulated juices on the plate to the sauce. Simmer, uncovered, over medium heat until the chicken is cooked through, 1 to 2 minutes. Stir in the cilantro.

4 SERVINGS

HONEYED CRANBERRY CHICKEN

Dried cranberries, which are becoming more widely available all the time, make an elegant tart-sweet sauce for chicken breasts.

 1 cup dried cranberries
 6 skinless, boneless chicken breast halves
 $3/4$ teaspoon salt
 $1/2$ teaspoon freshly ground pepper
 5 tablespoons butter
 $1/3$ cup chopped shallots
 3 tablespoons honey

1. Pour $1\frac{3}{4}$ cups boiling water over the dried cranberries and set aside to steep. Pound the chicken breasts slightly to flatten evenly. Season with $\frac{1}{4}$ teaspoon each salt and pepper.

2. Heat the butter in a large frying pan. Add the chicken breasts and cook over medium-high heat, turning once, until golden brown, about 2 minutes per side.

3. Reduce the heat to medium-low. Add the shallots to the pan and cook, stirring, for 30 seconds. Add the cranberries with their soaking liquid, raise the heat to high and boil, uncovered, for 2 minutes. Stir in the honey and continue to cook until the chicken is white but still moist in the center, about 2 minutes longer.

4. With the back of a fork, mash some of the cranberries into the sauce to help thicken it. Season with the remaining salt and pepper. Spoon the sauce and cranberries over the chicken and serve.

6 SERVINGS

MAPLE-MUSTARD CHICKEN SAUTÉ

Smoky-sweet maple syrup, savory leaf sage and tangy mustard combine to create this smooth and delicious sauce. A baked sweet potato and whole green beans would complement the chicken beautifully.

> 1 pound thinly sliced chicken cutlets
> Salt and freshly ground pepper
> 3 tablespoons butter
> 2 teaspoons crumbled dried sage leaves or 1 teaspoon powdered sage
> ¼ cup maple syrup
> 2 teaspoons Dijon mustard

1. Season the chicken cutlets with salt and pepper. Heat the butter in a large frying pan. Add the chicken and cook over medium heat until lightly browned and cooked through, about 2 minutes per side. Remove to a plate, leaving the drippings in the pan.

2. Add ⅔ cup water to the frying pan and bring to a boil, stirring up any browned bits on the bottom of the pan. Add the sage and maple syrup and boil, uncovered, until the sauce is slightly reduced and thickened, 1 to 2 minutes. Whisk in the mustard.

3. Return the chicken and any accumulated juices to the pan, heat through and serve.

4 SERVINGS

CHICKEN MARSALA

1 pound thinly sliced chicken cutlets
  Salt and freshly ground pepper
¼ cup olive oil
3 tablespoons chopped shallots
1 cup Marsala wine
1 medium lemon

1. Season the chicken cutlets with salt and pepper. Heat 3 tablespoons of the oil in a large frying pan. Add the chicken and cook over medium-high heat, turning once, until the chicken is browned and cooked through, about 1½ minutes per side. Remove to a plate, leaving the drippings in the pan.

2. Heat the remaining 1 tablespoon of oil in the pan. Add the shallots and cook over medium heat, stirring, for 1 minute. Add the Marsala and 2 tablespoons water. Bring to a boil over high heat, scraping up any brown bits from the bottom of the pan. Boil the sauce for 2 minutes, to reduce and thicken slightly. Reduce the heat to medium-low.

3. Cut the lemon in half and squeeze 2 teaspoons of juice from one half into the sauce. Season the sauce with salt and pepper to taste. Return the chicken and any accumulated juices to the pan and simmer for 1 minute to heat through.

4. Meanwhile, thinly slice the other lemon half. Garnish each serving with a slice of lemon.

4 SERVINGS

MEDITERRANEAN CHICKEN WITH ARTICHOKES

Marinated artichoke hearts are one of those prepared products that pack a big flavor wallop, because the marinade is full of Mediterranean seasonings. Orzo or other small pasta and a tomato salad would make nice side dishes.

    4 skinless, boneless chicken breast halves
       (about 5 ounces each)
       Freshly ground black pepper
    1 jar (6 ounces) marinated artichoke hearts
    1 cup chicken broth
    $^1/_2$ to $^3/_4$ teaspoon dried hot red pepper flakes
    2 tablespoons lemon juice

1. Pound the chicken breasts slightly to flatten evenly. Season with the pepper. Drain the artichoke hearts, reserving the marinade.

2. Heat $^1/_4$ cup of the artichoke marinade in a large frying pan. Add the chicken breasts and cook over medium heat until lightly browned, about 2 minutes per side.

3. Add the artichokes, chicken broth and red pepper flakes to the pan. Pour in the remaining marinade. Cover and cook over medium heat until the chicken is white in the center but still moist, about 5 minutes. Add the lemon juice. If the sauce is too liquid, boil uncovered for 1 minute to reduce slightly.

4 SERVINGS

CHICKEN NEAPOLITAN WITH SAUSAGE AND PEPPERS

Spicy-hot Italian sausage adds zip to this flavorful southern Italian specialty. Serve with pasta and a salad of sliced tomatoes dressed with olive oil and balsamic vinegar.

3/4 pound hot Italian link sausage
1 1/2 pounds skinless, boneless chicken breasts
  2 medium onions
  2 medium green bell peppers
  3 tablespoons olive oil

1. Cut the sausage into 1/2-inch slices. Cut the chicken breasts crosswise into 1/2-inch strips. Slice the onions. Cut the peppers into 1/2-inch strips.

2. Heat the oil in a large frying pan or flameproof casserole. Add the sausage and cook over medium-high heat, stirring, until the sausage is beginning to brown, about 3 minutes.

3. Add the chicken, onion and pepper strips to the frying pan and cook, stirring frequently, for 3 minutes. Add 1/3 cup water, cover the pan, reduce the heat to medium and cook, stirring once or twice, until the sausage is no longer pink, the chicken is white in the center and the vegetables are tender, about 4 minutes.

6 TO 8 SERVINGS

CHICKEN NIÇOISE

If you can find imported pitted black olives, by all means use them here for added flavor. If not, then the canned domestic variety will do just fine. Pasta tossed with olive oil and a green vegetable such as steamed broccoli are perfect accompaniments.

4 skinless, boneless chicken breast halves
   (about 5 ounces each)
   Salt and freshly ground pepper
3 garlic cloves
3 tablespoons olive oil
1 can (14 to 16 ounces) Italian-style stewed tomatoes with juice
1 can (2 ounces) sliced black olives (about 1/2 cup)

1. Pound the chicken breasts slightly to flatten evenly and season lightly with salt and pepper. Chop the garlic.

2. Heat the oil in a large frying pan. Add the chicken breasts and cook over medium-high heat until browned, about 2 minutes per side.

3. Reduce the heat to medium. Add the chopped garlic and cook, stirring frequently, until softened and fragrant, about 1 minute. Add the tomatoes with their juice. Drain the olives and add them to the pan. Cook, uncovered, spooning the tomato juices over the chicken, until the chicken is cooked through and the sauce is somewhat reduced and thickened, about 5 minutes. Season with salt and pepper to taste. To serve, spoon the tomato-olive sauce over the chicken.

4 SERVINGS

CHICKEN PAPRIKASH

Imported sweet Hungarian paprika adds a wonderful flavor to this sauce, but ordinary paprika works just fine, too. Poppy seed noodles and braised green cabbage would be perfect partners.

1 pound thinly sliced chicken cutlets
  Salt and freshly ground pepper
1 tablespoon paprika
1 medium onion
3 tablespoons vegetable oil
3/4 cup sour cream

1. Season both sides of the chicken cutlets with salt, pepper and 1½ teaspoons of the paprika. Chop the onion.

2. Heat 2 tablespoons of the oil in a large frying pan. Add the chicken and cook over medium heat until golden brown and cooked through, about 2 minutes per side. Remove to a serving plate and cover with foil to keep warm.

3. Add the remaining 1 tablespoon of oil to the drippings in the pan. Add the chopped onion and the remaining 1½ teaspoons paprika, and cook over medium heat, stirring frequently, until softened and lightly browned, 3 to 4 minutes.

4. Remove the pan from the heat and stir in the sour cream and 2 tablespoons warm water until smooth. Season with salt and pepper to taste. Pour the sauce over the chicken and serve at once.

4 SERVINGS

PARMESAN CHICKEN

Garnish this crusty, pan-fried chicken with a lemon wedge and parsley sprigs, and offer French fries and a tomato salad on the side.

4 skinless, boneless chicken breast halves
   (about 5 ounces each)
1 egg
$2/3$ cup dry bread crumbs with Italian seasonings
2 tablespoons grated Parmesan cheese
$1/4$ cup olive oil

1. Pound the chicken breasts to flatten to an even $1/2$-inch thickness. In a shallow dish, whisk the egg with 1 tablespoon of water. In another dish, combine the bread crumbs and cheese.

2. Dip the chicken breasts in the egg and dredge in the Parmesan bread crumbs to coat both sides.

3. Heat the oil in a large frying pan. Add the chicken breasts and cook over medium heat until crusty brown on the outside and white but still moist inside, 4 to 5 minutes per side.

4 SERVINGS

CHICKEN PATTIES WITH THYME

Buy lean ground chicken breast meat or grind it at home in the food processor by following our simple directions.

2 slices of firm-textured white bread
1¼ pounds skinless, boneless chicken breasts
½ teaspoon salt
½ teaspoon freshly ground pepper
1½ teaspoons dried thyme leaves
4 tablespoons butter
1 cup chicken broth

1. Break the bread into pieces and process in a food processor to make coarse crumbs. Transfer to a plate.

2. Trim the chicken and cut into 1-inch chunks. In the food processor, combine the chicken with the salt, pepper and 1 teaspoon thyme. Pulse until the chicken is coarsely ground; do not process to a paste. Shape into 4 patties, each about 4 inches in diameter.

3. Dredge the chicken patties in the crumbs, patting so they adhere. Heat the butter in a large frying pan. Add the patties and cook over medium heat until deep golden brown on the bottom, about 4 minutes. Turn and cook until browned on the second side and cooked through, 3 to 4 minutes. Remove to a warm platter.

4. Add the broth and remaining ½ teaspoon thyme to the pan. Boil over high heat, stirring, until the sauce is slightly reduced, about 1 minute. Pour the sauce over the patties before serving.

4 SERVINGS

PECAN CHICKEN CUTLETS

Ground pecans make a rich, crunchy crust for sautéed chicken cutlets. Serve with baked sweet potatoes and steamed greens. Any fruit vinegar can be used in place of the raspberry suggested here.

1 pound thinly sliced chicken cutlets
    Salt and freshly ground pepper
1 cup pecans
2 tablespoons flour
¼ cup vegetable oil
3 tablespoons raspberry vinegar

1. Season the chicken cutlets with salt and pepper. In a food processor, combine the pecans and flour. Process in pulses until the nuts are finely chopped but not oily. Transfer to a plate.

2. Dredge the chicken in the pecan flour, pressing the nuts into the meat. Heat the oil in a large frying pan. Add the cutlets and cook over medium heat, turning once, until the pecan crust is browned and the chicken is cooked through, about 3 minutes per side. Transfer to dinner plates or a serving platter.

3. Pour ¼ cup water and the vinegar into the pan. Bring to a boil, reduce the heat and simmer for 1 minute. Pour the sauce over the chicken and serve.

4 SERVINGS

CHICKEN PICCATA

Originally popularized in Italy with veal, this piquant sauce is also wonderful with thinly sliced chicken or turkey cutlets. Steamed broccoli and rice would make a lovely meal.

1 pound thinly sliced chicken cutlets
   Salt and freshly ground pepper
2 garlic cloves
2 lemons
3 tablespoons olive oil
1 cup chicken broth

1. Season the chicken cutlets with salt and pepper. Finely chop the garlic. Grate 1 teaspoon of the colored zest and squeeze 3 tablespoons of juice from 1½ lemons. Cut 4 thin slices from the remaining lemon half and set aside.

2. Heat the oil in a large frying pan. Add the chicken and cook over medium-high heat, turning once, until lightly browned, about 1½ minutes per side.

3. Reduce the heat to medium. Push the chicken to one side of the pan, add the garlic and cook, stirring until softened but not browned, about 1 minute. Add the lemon zest, lemon juice and chicken broth. Bring to a boil, reduce the heat to medium and simmer, uncovered, until the chicken is cooked through, about 3 minutes. Garnish with the lemon slices.

4 SERVINGS

CHICKEN WITH RED PEPPER SAUCE

Roasted red peppers packed in jars are one of the handiest ready-prepared products we know. Here they are pureed to make a spectacular sauce for chicken.

6 skinless, boneless chicken breast halves
    Salt and freshly ground pepper
3 garlic cloves
3 tablespoons olive oil
1 large jar (12 ounces) roasted red peppers
1/4 cup heavy cream or milk

1. Pound the chicken breasts slightly to flatten evenly. Season with salt and pepper. Chop the garlic.

2. Heat the oil in a large frying pan. Add the chicken breasts and cook over medium-high heat until browned on the outside and white in the center but still moist, 3 to 4 minutes per side.

3. Meanwhile, drain the roasted peppers into a sieve, rinse and drain well. In a food processor, combine the roasted peppers with the cream, 1/4 teaspoon salt and 1/8 teaspoon black pepper. Process until smooth. Taste and add more salt and pepper if needed.

4. When the chicken is cooked, remove it to a serving platter. Add the garlic to the pan and cook, stirring, until softened and fragrant, about 1 minute. Pour the pepper puree into the pan and heat through. Spoon the red pepper sauce over the chicken and serve.

6 SERVINGS

CHICKEN SALTIMBOCCA

Classically made with veal, *saltimbocca*, loosely translated as "jump into the mouth," is an Italian specialty that is so good that you wish for it to do just that. We like to serve this with steamed zucchini and noodles or pasta tossed with butter and garlic.

1 pound thinly sliced chicken cutlets
 Freshly ground pepper
1 tablespoon dried leaf sage
4 ounces mozzarella cheese
3 tablespoons olive oil
2 ounces very thinly sliced prosciutto

1. Sprinkle both sides of the chicken cutlets with the pepper and then with the sage, rubbing it into the meat. Thinly slice the mozzarella or shred it coarsely in a food processor or on the large holes of a hand grater. Or to save time, buy the cheese shredded.

2. Heat the oil in a large frying pan. Add the chicken and cook over medium heat for about 1½ minutes on the first side. Turn the chicken over; layer on the prosciutto and then the cheese to cover the cooked side of the chicken. Reduce the heat to medium-low, cover the pan and cook until the cheese is melted and the chicken is cooked through, about 2 minutes.

4 SERVINGS

SESAME CHICKEN NUGGETS

You can use either chicken breasts or thinly sliced cutlets to make these delectable nuggets, which, incidentally, also make a terrific hors d'oeuvre. For supper, serve them with mashed potatoes and a big green salad.

    1 pound skinless, boneless chicken breasts
      Salt and freshly ground pepper
  1/2 cup sesame seeds
    1 medium lemon
    3 tablespoons vegetable oil
    2 teaspoons sesame oil

1. Cut the chicken crosswise into strips 1/2 inch wide and season with salt and pepper. Put the sesame seeds into a plastic or paper bag and shake the chicken strips in the seeds to coat. Quarter the lemon lengthwise into 4 wedges.

2. Heat the vegetable oil and the sesame oil together in a large frying pan. Add the chicken, in one layer if possible, and cook over medium heat until golden brown on the bottom, 2 to 3 minutes. Turn the strips with tongs and cook on the other side until the chicken is cooked through, about 2 minutes. Regulate the heat if necessary to make sure the sesame seeds don't burn.

3. Serve the sesame chicken nuggets, garnished with a wedge of lemon.

4 SERVINGS

SOUTHERN-STYLE CUTLETS WITH CREAM GRAVY

Cornmeal adds its wonderful texture and flavor to this crunchy coating for cutlets, and the rich pan gravy is icing on the cake. Buttermilk biscuits and a spinach salad would be welcome accompaniments.

1 pound thinly sliced chicken cutlets
  Salt and freshly ground pepper
1½ teaspoons poultry seasoning
  ½ cup yellow cornmeal
  ¼ cup corn oil
  1 cup light cream or half-and-half

1. Season the chicken cutlets with salt and pepper and sprinkle with the poultry seasoning. Spread the cornmeal on a plate and dredge the chicken in the cornmeal to coat both sides. Shake off any excess.

2. Heat the oil in a large frying pan. Add the chicken and cook over medium heat until golden brown and cooked through, about 3 minutes per side. Remove the chicken to a serving plate.

3. Add the cream to the pan drippings. Bring to a boil, stirring up the browned bits from the bottom of the pan. Boil, uncovered, stirring often, until the sauce is slightly reduced and thickened, about 1½ minutes. Pour the gravy over the chicken and serve.

4 SERVINGS

SUMMER CHICKEN SAUTÉ

Corn kernels and chopped tomato add a summery note to this colorful chicken preparation. Add a big salad of summer greens and crusty bread to complete the meal.

    4 skinless, boneless chicken breast halves
      (about 5 ounces each)
      Salt and freshly ground pepper
    1 large ripe tomato
    4 tablespoons butter
1½ cups thawed frozen or canned corn kernels
  ¼ cup minced chives or green onion tops

1. Pound the chicken breasts slightly to flatten evenly and season with salt and pepper. Peel and core the tomato, squeeze out the seeds and coarsely chop.

2. Heat the butter in a large frying pan. Add the chicken breasts and cook over medium heat, turning once, until golden, about 2 minutes per side.

3. Add the chopped tomato, corn kernels and ¼ cup water to the frying pan. Cover, reduce the heat to medium and cook until the chicken is white in the center but still moist and the corn is tender, about 5 minutes.

4. Stir in the chives before serving.

4 SERVINGS

CHICKEN WITH SUN-DRIED TOMATOES AND VODKA

Sun-dried tomatoes are packed in oil usually flavored with garlic and herbs, so the oil is a wonderful cooking medium. Fettuccine noodles and sautéed broccoli rabe would complete this rather sophisticated chicken dish very nicely.

6 skinless, boneless chicken breast halves
   (about 5 ounces each)
   Freshly ground pepper
$^1/_2$ cup marinated sun-dried tomatoes, plus $2^1/_2$ tablespoons of
   the oil
 1 cup heavy cream
$^1/_3$ cup vodka
 1 teaspoon dried basil

1. Pound the chicken breasts slightly to flatten evenly. Season generously with pepper. Cut the sun-dried tomatoes into thin slivers.

2. Heat the tomato oil in a large frying pan. Add the chicken breasts and cook over medium heat, turning once, until well browned, about 3 minutes per side.

3. Pour in the cream. Add the vodka, sun-dried tomatoes and basil. Bring to a boil, reduce the heat to medium-low, cover and cook until the chicken is white in the center but still moist, 3 to 4 minutes.

6 SERVINGS

TARRAGON CHICKEN SAUTÉ

Tarragon and chicken have a natural affinity, so here we use this bright-tasting herb in a classically elegant wine and cream sauce. Served with asparagus and tiny new red potatoes, this makes a lovely spring dinner for two.

$1/2$ pound thinly sliced chicken cutlets
　　Salt and freshly ground pepper
$1 1/2$ tablespoons butter
$1/3$ cup dry white wine
$1/4$ cup heavy or whipping cream
$3/4$ teaspoon dried tarragon

1. Season the chicken cutlets with salt and pepper. Heat the butter in a large frying pan. Add the chicken and cook over medium heat, turning once, until the chicken is lightly browned and cooked through, about 2 minutes per side. Remove to a plate, leaving the drippings in the pan.

2. Add the wine to the pan, stirring to scrape up any browned bits on the bottom. Boil, uncovered, for 1 minute. Add the cream and tarragon and boil until the sauce is slightly reduced and thickened, about 1 minute longer. Season with salt and pepper to taste.

3. Return the chicken and any accumulated juices to the sauce and simmer for 1 minute to heat through.

2 SERVINGS

CHICKEN WITH TONNATO SAUCE

This sautéed chicken, cut into angled slices and topped with tonnato (or tuna) sauce, makes a perfect summer buffet dish. Serve with a pasta salad, sliced tomatoes and French bread.

6 skinless, boneless chicken breast halves
   Salt
$3/4$ teaspoon freshly ground pepper
3 tablespoons olive oil
1 can ($6^1/8$ ounces) tuna packed in oil
$3/4$ cup mayonnaise
2 tablespoons tiny (nonpareil) capers

1. Pound the chicken breasts to flatten slightly. Season with salt and $1/2$ teaspoon pepper. Heat the olive oil in a large frying pan, add the chicken and cook over medium heat, turning once, until the chicken is browned on the outside and white in the center but still moist, 3 to 4 minutes per side. Remove to a plate and let cool.

2. In a blender or food processor, combine the tuna and its oil, the mayonnaise, 5 teaspoons of the capers and the remaining $1/4$ teaspoon pepper. Process until the sauce is smooth. Add 3 tablespoons of water and process again.

3. Cut the chicken crosswise on an angle into thin slices about 1 inch wide and place on a serving platter. Spoon the sauce over the chicken to coat. If made ahead, cover and refrigerate. Serve cool, garnished with the remaining capers.

8 SERVINGS

TRATTORIA CHICKEN AND CAPELLINI

The newly available diced canned tomatoes labeled "pasta ready" are pleasingly seasoned with herbs, garlic and a touch of olive oil. If you can't find them, substitute good-quality Italian-style stewed tomatoes.

2 bunches of arugula
4 ounces thinly sliced prosciutto
1 pound thinly sliced chicken cutlets
2 cans (14½ ounces each) "pasta ready" diced tomatoes
1 pound capellini
   Freshly ground pepper

1. Wash and dry the arugula, then thinly slice. Cut the prosciutto and the chicken into thin strips. Bring a large pot of salted water to a boil.

2. In a large frying pan, cook the prosciutto, stirring, over medium-high heat for 1 minute, or just until the fat is rendered. Add the chicken and cook, tossing, until lightly browned, about 2 minutes. Add the arugula and toss for 30 seconds. Add the tomatoes and juices and simmer for 2 minutes.

3. Meanwhile, cook the capellini in the boiling salted water until tender but still firm, about 5 minutes. Drain in a colander, then toss with the sauce in the skillet. Season generously with black pepper.

4 TO 6 SERVINGS

TUSCAN CHICKEN WITH
SWEET PEPPERS AND GARLIC

This hearty chicken dish is wonderful with pasta tossed with a little olive oil and Parmesan cheese and served with steamed broccoli spears.

4 skinless, boneless chicken breast halves
  Salt and freshly ground pepper
1 large red bell pepper
3 tablespoons extra virgin olive oil
2 garlic cloves, finely chopped
2 tablespoons balsamic vinegar

1. Pound the chicken breasts slightly to flatten evenly. Season with salt and pepper. Seed the bell pepper and cut into $1/2$-inch strips.

2. Heat the oil in a large frying pan. Add the chicken breasts and cook over medium heat, turning once, until golden brown, about 2 minutes per side. Add the bell pepper strips to the pan, cover and reduce the heat to medium-low. Cook until the peppers are tender and the chicken is white to the center but still moist, about 3 minutes.

3. Add the garlic to the pan. Cook, uncovered, stirring, until softened, about 1 minute. Stir in the vinegar and 1 tablespoon water and serve.

4 SERVINGS

WILD MUSHROOM CHICKEN SAUTÉ

Use any combination of wild mushrooms that happen to be in season and available in the market—shiitakes, oyster mushrooms, chanterelles. Or you can use a mix of wild and domestic mushrooms. Noodles tossed with poppy seeds and steamed red cabbage would make appropriately autumnal accompaniments.

4 skinless, boneless chicken breast halves
   (about 5 ounces each)
   Salt and freshly ground pepper
12 ounces fresh wild mushrooms
4 tablespoons butter
⅓ cup chopped shallots
1 cup dry white wine

1. Pound the chicken breasts slightly to flatten evenly. Season with salt and pepper. Wipe the mushrooms with a damp paper towel to remove any dirt. Slice the mushrooms.

2. Heat the butter in a large frying pan. Add the chicken breasts and cook over medium-high heat, turning once, or until golden brown, about 2 minutes per side. Push the chicken to one side of the pan, add the mushrooms and shallots and stir to coat with butter. Add the wine and stir again. Cover the pan and cook over medium heat for 4 minutes. Uncover and cook until the chicken is cooked through and the liquid is slightly reduced, about 1 minute longer. Taste and season with salt and pepper if necessary. Spoon the mushrooms over the chicken to serve.

4 SERVINGS

4 STIR-FRIES

Although stir-frying is best known in connection with Chinese cooking, the technique has been enthusiastically embraced by Americans, and the quick searing over high heat is eminently well suited to boneless chicken breasts.

The secret to a successful quick and easy stir-fry lies in preparing all the ingredients before you even begin to think about heating the oil. The chicken should always be cut uniformly. When cutting into thin strips, we suggest first cutting the breast halves in half *horizontally* before slicing them into thin strips approximately ¼ inch wide. (If you happen to have them on hand, thinly sliced chicken breast cutlets are very easy to cut into strips.) And make sure that all vegetables are chopped or cut up and that any sauce ingredients are pre-measured or prepared, so that when you start cooking, you can work very quickly without pause.

A traditional Chinese wok offers the ideal shape and size for this cooking method and has the advantage of requiring less oil than a flat-bottomed pan. If you don't have a wok, a large well-seasoned or nonstick frying pan can be used.

If this is your first foray into stir-frying, you'll quickly master this easy cooking technique. Just make sure the oil and pan are quite hot before you begin. Then, if you stir almost constantly over high heat, you'll find the food will cook nicely without scorching or steaming.

CHICKEN, ASPARAGUS AND ORANGE STIR-FRY

1 pound skinless, boneless chicken breasts
$^3/_4$ teaspoon salt
$^1/_4$ teaspoon freshly ground pepper
1 pound asparagus
2 oranges
8 green onions
$3^1/_2$ tablespoons vegetable oil

1. Cut the chicken into thin strips and season with $^1/_4$ teaspoon of salt and $^1/_8$ teaspoon of the pepper. Cut the asparagus into 1-inch lengths, discarding tough bottoms. Grate 2 teaspoons of colored zest and squeeze $^1/_2$ cup of juice from $1^1/_2$ oranges. Cut 6 thin slices from the remaining orange half and cut the slices in half. Thinly slice the green onions.

2. Heat 2 tablespoons of the oil in a wok or large frying pan. Add the chicken and stir-fry over high heat until just cooked through, 2 to 3 minutes. Remove to a plate.

3. Add the remaining $1^1/_2$ tablespoons of oil to the pan and reduce the heat to medium-high. Add the asparagus and stir-fry until just tender, 2 to 3 minutes.

4. Return the chicken to the pan. Add $^1/_2$ cup water, the orange zest, orange juice, orange slices and remaining salt and pepper. Cook until heated through, about 1 minute longer. Stir in the green onions and serve.

4 SERVINGS

CHICKEN AND BROCCOLI STIR-FRY

Of course, you can buy a whole head of broccoli, trim it into florets and thinly slice the stems. But these days food stores cater to busy cooks with pre-cut broccoli florets. Look for them in the produce or salad bar section of your supermarket.

3/4 pound skinless, boneless chicken breasts
    Freshly ground pepper
1 pound broccoli florets
3 garlic cloves
3 tablespoons vegetable oil
2 tablespoons soy sauce

1. Cut the chicken breasts into thin strips and season with the pepper. If not already prepared, cut the broccoli into 1½-inch florets. Finely chop the garlic.

2. Heat 2 tablespoons of the oil in a wok or large frying pan. Add the chicken and stir-fry over high heat until barely cooked through, 2 to 3 minutes. Remove to a plate.

3. Heat the remaining 1 tablespoon of oil in the wok. Add the broccoli, reduce the heat to medium-high and stir-fry for 2 minutes. Add the garlic and stir-fry for 30 seconds.

4. Return the chicken to the pan. Add 3/4 cup water and the soy sauce. Bring to a boil, reduce the heat to medium-high and boil, stirring frequently, until the broccoli is crisp-tender and the chicken is cooked through, about 2 minutes.

3 TO 4 SERVINGS

STIR-FRIED CHICKEN WITH BABY CORN AND RED PEPPERS

Baby corn only a few inches long is a specialty Chinese item that's now sold in jars or cans with the other Asian ingredients in most supermarkets. In addition to tasting very good, it's always a conversation piece.

1 pound skinless, boneless chicken breasts
   Salt and freshly ground pepper
1 large red bell pepper
8 green onions
1 can (14 ounces) baby corn
3 tablespoons vegetable oil

1. Cut the chicken breasts into thin strips and season with salt and pepper. Cut the red pepper into thin slices and thinly slice the green onions. Drain the corn and rinse in a strainer.

2. Heat the oil in a wok or large frying pan. Add the chicken and red pepper and stir-fry over high heat until just cooked through, 2 to 3 minutes. Add the green onions, baby corn and ½ cup water. Cook, stirring, until heated through, 1 to 2 minutes.

4 SERVINGS

CASHEW CHICKEN AND SNOW PEAS

If you prefer to use unsalted or raw cashew nuts in this recipe, season with salt to taste at the end of the cooking time.

3/4 pound skinless, boneless chicken breasts
    Freshly ground pepper
1/2 pound snow peas
 3 garlic cloves
 3 tablespoons peanut or vegetable oil
1/2 cup salted roasted cashews

1. Cut the chicken into thin strips and season with pepper. Remove stems and strings from the snow peas and cut them in half diagonally if they are very large. Finely chop the garlic.

2. Heat 2 tablespoons of the oil in a wok or large frying pan. Over high heat add the chicken and stir-fry until just cooked through, 2 to 3 minutes. Remove to a plate.

3. Add the remaining 1 tablespoon of oil to the wok and stir-fry the snow peas over high heat for 1 minute. Reduce the heat to medium. Add the garlic and cashews and cook, stirring, for 1 minute.

4. Return the chicken to the pan, add 1/2 cup water and simmer until heated through, about 1 minute.

3 TO 4 SERVINGS

Coriander Chicken and Apple Stir-Fry

Coriander seed, which has a mild, almost citrusy flavor, is a wonderful seasoning for both chicken and apple. This stir-fry is terrific with steamed couscous, along with a salad of sliced tomatoes and cucumbers drizzled with yogurt-mint dressing.

1 pound skinless, boneless chicken breasts
  Salt and freshly ground pepper
4 teaspoons ground coriander
2 firm red apples, such as Empire or Red Delicious
1 medium onion
3$^1/_2$ tablespoons vegetable oil

1. Cut the chicken into thin strips, season with salt and pepper and sprinkle on all sides with the ground coriander. Core the apples but do not peel. Cut them into $^1/_4$-inch slices. Thinly slice the onion.

2. Heat 2 tablespoons of the oil in a wok or large frying pan over high heat. Add the chicken and stir-fry until just cooked through, 2 to 3 minutes. Remove to a plate.

3. Add the remaining 1$^1/_2$ tablespoons of oil to the pan, add the apples and onion and stir-fry over medium-high heat until lightly browned, about 2 minutes.

4. Return the chicken to the pan, add $^1/_2$ cup water and simmer until heated through, about 1 minute.

4 SERVINGS

CHICKEN STIR-FRY WITH GARLIC AND GREENS

Any type of frozen greens—turnip, mustard or collards—will be fine in this Southern-style stir-fry. Serve it with plain white rice, a beet salad and corn muffins.

1 pound skinless, boneless chicken breasts
  Salt and freshly ground pepper
1 package (10 ounces) frozen greens
4 garlic cloves
3 tablespoons vegetable oil
1/2 teaspoon Tabasco sauce, or to taste

1. Cut the chicken into thin strips and season lightly with salt and pepper. Thaw the greens in a microwave on High for 1 to 2 minutes. Drain greens in a colander and press out most of the liquid. Chop the garlic.

2. Heat the oil in a wok or large frying pan over high heat. Add the chicken and stir-fry until just cooked through, 2 to 3 minutes. Reduce the heat to medium, add the garlic and cook, stirring, for 1 minute.

3. Add the greens and cook, stirring, until tender, about 2 minutes. Season with the Tabasco and salt to taste and serve.

4 SERVINGS

GINGER CHICKEN AND MIXED VEGETABLES

There are several good combinations of frozen stir-fry vegetables available in supermarkets. Use whichever mixture appeals to you, and serve the stir-fry over quick-cooking brown rice.

1 package (1 pound) frozen mixed stir-fry vegetables
1 pound skinless, boneless chicken breasts
$\frac{1}{2}$ teaspoon salt
$\frac{1}{4}$ teaspoon freshly ground pepper
3 garlic cloves
3 tablespoons vegetable oil
2 tablespoons minced fresh ginger

1. Thaw the vegetables in a microwave, if necessary. Drain well. Cut the chicken breasts into $\frac{1}{2}$-inch dice and season with half the salt and pepper. Finely chop the garlic.

2. Heat the oil in a wok or large frying pan. Add the chicken and stir-fry over high heat until almost cooked through, about 2 minutes. Add the garlic and ginger and cook until fragrant, 30 to 60 seconds.

3. Add the vegetables, $\frac{3}{4}$ cup water and the remaining salt and pepper. Bring to a boil and cook, stirring often, until the vegetables are tender and most of the liquid has evaporated, 2 to 3 minutes.

4 SERVINGS

HOISIN CHICKEN STIR-FRY

Chinese hoisin sauce is a wonderful staple to have on hand not only for stir-fries but also as a barbecue sauce. As is almost always the case, it's worth it to pay a little more for the best quality.

1½ pounds skinless, boneless chicken breasts
   5 medium carrots
   2 medium green bell peppers
   5 tablespoons vegetable oil
¾ cup hoisin sauce

1. Cut the chicken into ½- to ¾-inch dice. Peel the carrots and slice thinly on an angle. Cut the peppers into ½-inch squares.

2. Heat 3 tablespoons of the oil in a wok or large frying pan. Add the chicken and stir-fry over high heat until almost cooked through, 2 to 3 minutes. Remove to a plate.

3. Add the remaining 2 tablespoons oil to the pan and reduce the heat to medium-high. Add the carrots and peppers and stir-fry until crisp-tender, about 2 minutes.

4. Return the chicken to the pan. Add 1 cup water and stir in the hoisin sauce. Bring to a boil, reduce the heat to medium and simmer until the chicken is cooked through and the vegetables are just tender, about 3 minutes.

6 SERVINGS

LEMON CHICKEN WITH GREEN ONIONS

Lemon and chicken are perfect partners in this delicious stir-fry. In keeping with the delicacy of this dish, we recommend serving it with a thin pasta, such as capellini or spaghettini.

1 pound skinless, boneless chicken breasts
$1/2$ teaspoon salt
$1/4$ teaspoon freshly ground pepper
2 large lemons
8 green onions
2 teaspoons cornstarch
3 tablespoons vegetable oil

1. Cut the chicken into thin strips and season with salt and pepper. Grate 1 teaspoon of colored zest and squeeze 3 tablespoons of juice from one of the lemons. Cut the second lemon into thin slices and halve the slices. Thinly slice the green onions. Dissolve the cornstarch in 1 cup of cold water.

2. Heat the oil in a wok or large frying pan. Add the chicken and stir-fry over high heat until just cooked through, 2 to 3 minutes. Add the lemon zest, lemon juice, lemon slices and green onions. Stir in the cornstarch and water mixture. Bring to a boil, stirring, until the sauce is translucent and thickened, 1 to 2 minutes.

3 TO 4 SERVINGS

PEANUT CHICKEN STIR-FRY

This is a 5 in 10 version of the traditional *kung pao* chicken. If you like hot food, omit the black pepper and add instead ¼ to ½ teaspoon crushed hot red pepper with the garlic (though that will be a sixth ingredient). Serve this particularly tasty peanut-flavored stir-fry over white rice, with a broccoli salad on the side.

    2 celery ribs
    1 pound skinless, boneless chicken breasts
      Freshly ground pepper
    3 garlic cloves
    3 tablespoons peanut or vegetable oil
  ³/₄ cup dry-roasted peanuts

1. Cut the celery into ½-inch pieces. Cut the chicken breasts into ½-inch dice and season with pepper. Finely chop the garlic.

2. Heat the oil in a wok or large frying pan. Add the celery and stir-fry over high heat for 1 minute. Add the chicken and stir-fry until almost cooked through, about 3 minutes. Add the garlic and continue to cook, stirring, 1 minute. Add ½ cup water and cook for 1 minute longer.

3. Stir in the peanuts and serve.

4 SERVINGS

SWEET-AND-SOUR CHICKEN AND PEPPER STIR-FRY

A good-quality bottled sweet-and-sour sauce, with its interesting balance of flavors (usually from pureed preserves and rice vinegar), has a lot of appeal. Serve this stir-fry with rice and a bowl of crispy noodles to sprinkle on top.

1 pound skinless, boneless chicken breasts
   Freshly ground pepper
1 medium red bell pepper
1 large onion
3 tablespoons vegetable oil
1 cup sweet-and-sour sauce

1. Cut the chicken into thin strips and season with the pepper. Cut the red pepper into ¼-inch slices. Cut the onion into ¼-inch slices.

2. Heat 2 tablespoons of the oil in a wok or large frying pan over high heat. Add the chicken and stir-fry until just cooked through, 2 to 3 minutes. Remove to a plate.

3. Add the remaining 1 tablespoon of oil to the wok and reduce the heat to medium-high. Add the pepper and onion and stir-fry for 2 minutes.

4. Return the chicken to the pan. Add ½ cup water and the sweet-and-sour sauce. Simmer, stirring, until heated through, 2 minutes.

3 TO 4 SERVINGS

5 BAKED AND BROILED

Skinless, boneless chicken breasts do very nicely under the broiler, especially if they are first flattened to an even thickness (or if thin cutlets are used) and the chicken is protected and flavored with an assertively seasoned sauce. The results are similar to those obtained on an outdoor grill, but without the fuss and time spent in building a fire. In fact, many of the recipes in our grilling chapter are easily adaptable to the broiler, and those in this chapter are generally just as good cooked over a grill. Some special touches, though, make these perfectly suited to the overhead heat source of the broiler. For example, fresh fruits, which are hard to turn on a grill, and tend to fall through the grates, are very pretty and taste fabulous when broiled to a caramelized sheen as part of Broiled Peachy Chicken or Broiled Apple and Sage Chicken.

Baking chicken in 10 minutes poses a challenge, but we've come up with some delightful—and delicious—surprises. Breaded or coated with crumbs, chicken bakes to a wonderful golden crisp exterior with a moist, juicy interior in just 8 minutes at 500 degrees F. The results are as varied as Crusty Cornbread Baked Chicken using packaged stuffing mix and a streamlined Quick Chicken Cordon Bleu with fresh French bread crumbs. All of these recipes offer old-fashioned goodness in a very modern 10 minutes or less.

BROILED APPLE AND SAGE CHICKEN

> 4 skinless, boneless chicken breast halves (about 5 ounces each)
> Salt and freshly ground pepper
> 1 large tart apple, such as Granny Smith
> 1/3 cup apple jelly
> 1 1/2 tablespoons white wine vinegar
> 1 1/2 tablespoons chopped fresh sage, or 1 1/2 teaspoons dried leaf sage

1. Preheat the broiler. Pound the chicken breasts slightly to flatten evenly. Season generously with salt and pepper. Core and cut the unpeeled apple into 1/4-inch slices.

2. In a small nonreactive saucepan, cook the jelly, vinegar and sage over medium-low heat, stirring occasionally, until the jelly is melted, about 2 minutes. Brush both sides of the chicken with some of the jelly mixture and place the chicken on a broiler pan.

3. Broil about 4 inches from the heat for 4 minutes. Brush with the jelly mixture. Turn the chicken, add the apple slices to the broiler pan and brush the chicken and the apples with more of the jelly mixture. Broil about 4 minutes longer, turning the chicken and apples once and basting both, until the chicken is golden on the outside and white but still moist in the center and the apples are glazed and softened.

4 SERVINGS

BACON AND CHEDDAR CHICKEN

Bacon and Cheddar is an all-time favorite flavor combination with both of our families. We particularly love this crispy, baked version and serve it often with a side of rigatoni tossed with broccoli florets and a mixed lettuce salad.

> 6 skinless, boneless chicken breast halves
>   (about 5 ounces each)
> 1½ cups dry bread crumbs seasoned with Italian herbs
>   1 egg, beaten
>   6 slices of bacon
>   1 cup shredded Cheddar cheese (4 ounces)

1. Preheat the oven to 500 degrees F. Pound the chicken breasts slightly to flatten evenly. Place the bread crumbs on a plate. In a shallow bowl, beat the egg with 2 tablespoons water. Dip the chicken in the egg mixture, then dredge in the bread crumbs to coat completely. Place the chicken on a baking sheet. Cut the bacon slices in half crosswise and place them on the baking sheet next to the chicken.

2. Bake until the chicken is white in the center but still juicy and the coating is golden brown, about 8 minutes.

3. Change the oven setting to broil. Sprinkle the cheese over the chicken and place the bacon slices on top. Blot up any bacon fat on the sheet with a paper towel. Broil about 4 inches from the heat until the cheese is melted, 30 to 60 seconds.

6 SERVINGS

BROILED BUFFALO CHICKEN

This takeoff on the popular spicy Buffalo wings has all the zip of the original but none of the mess of frying. If you want to serve them as appetizers, simply cut the chicken pieces into bite-size portions before broiling, then serve the blue cheese dressing on the side. In any case, celery sticks are the traditional accompaniment.

4 tablespoons melted butter
1/4 teaspoon cayenne pepper
1 tablespoon Tabasco or other hot sauce
1 1/4 pounds thinly sliced chicken cutlets
1/2 cup bottled chunky blue cheese salad dressing

1. Preheat the broiler. In a shallow dish, combine the butter, cayenne and 1 tablespoon Tabasco sauce. Mix well. Dip the chicken into the butter mixture to coat completely. Place on a broiler pan.

2. Broil 4 inches from the heat for about 6 minutes, until the chicken is golden outside and white but still moist in the center. Brush with any remaining sauce about halfway through the broiling time.

3. Serve the chicken with a spoonful of blue cheese dressing on top. Pass the bottle of Tabasco sauce around the table for those who really like it hot.

4 SERVINGS

QUICK CHICKEN CORDON BLEU

This highly unorthodox version of a favorite classic is delicious as
well as exceedingly quick and easy. Team it with an herbed rice
pilaf and asparagus for a lovely dinner.

4 skinless boneless chicken breast halves
   (about 5 ounces each)
3 slices of French bread (about 4 ounces total)
1/4 teaspoon freshly ground pepper
1 egg
4 thin slices of prosciutto or baked ham
1 cup shredded Swiss cheese

1. Preheat the oven to 500 degrees F. Pound the chicken slightly
to flatten evenly. In a food processor, grind the French bread into
fine crumbs; there will be about 1 cup. Add the pepper and process
a few seconds to blend. Turn the crumbs onto a plate.

2. In a wide, shallow bowl, beat the egg with 2 tablespoons water.
Dip the chicken into the egg mixture, then dredge in the bread
crumbs to coat completely. Place the chicken in a single layer on a
baking sheet.

3. Bake for about 8 minutes, until the chicken is white in the
center but still juicy and the crumb mixture is light golden brown.

4. Change the oven setting to broil. Top the chicken with the
prosciutto, then sprinkle with the cheese. Broil 4 inches from the
heat for about 1 minute, until the cheese is melted.

4 SERVINGS

CRUSTY CORNBREAD
BAKED CHICKEN

This is an ingenious way to use packaged stuffing mix. The recipe is also delicious with herb-seasoned stuffing. Serve this with green beans and creamed onions for a delicious traditional supper with friends.

8 skinless, boneless chicken breast halves (about 5 ounces each)
Freshly ground pepper
8 ounces (about 3½ cups) packaged cornbread stuffing mix
4 teaspoons dried sage
6 tablespoons melted butter

1. Preheat the oven to 500 degrees F. Pound the chicken breasts slightly to flatten evenly. Sprinkle generously with pepper. Crush the stuffing mix in a food processor to make fine crumbs. Add the sage and process a few seconds to mix. Turn the crumbs onto a plate.

2. Dip the chicken in the melted butter to coat completely, then dip into the crumbs, pressing to adhere all over. Place the breaded chicken on a baking sheet.

3. Bake for about 8 minutes, until the chicken is white in the center but still juicy and the coating is golden brown. If the crumbs aren't brown enough, place under the broiler for about 1 minute.

8 SERVINGS

BAKED CHICKEN DIABLO

The zesty, strong flavor of grainy mustard is tempered by whole wheat bread crumbs to make this nicely flavorful main course for entertaining, which goes well with lightly buttered spinach noodles and a salad of sliced tomatoes.

8 skinless, boneless chicken breast halves
   (about 5 ounces each)
2 garlic cloves
1/4 cup plus 2 tablespoons grainy Dijon mustard
1/4 cup plus 2 tablespoons olive oil
4 slices of whole wheat bread
1/2 teaspoon freshly ground pepper

1. Preheat the oven to 500 degrees F. Pound the chicken breasts slightly to flatten evenly. Mince the garlic. In a shallow dish, combine the garlic, mustard and olive oil. Whisk to blend well. In a food processor, grind the bread slices into fine crumbs; there will be about 2 cups. Turn the bread crumbs into a shallow bowl and toss with the pepper.

2. Dip the chicken into the mustard mixture to coat well. Then dredge in the bread crumbs to coat completely. Place on a baking sheet.

3. Bake for about 8 minutes, until the chicken is white in the center but still juicy and the crumb coating is golden brown. If the crumbs aren't brown enough, place under the broiler for another minute or so.

8 SERVINGS

BROILED GINGER AND
ORANGE MARMALADE CHICKEN

Because of the intensity of orange flavor here, it's worth looking for a good imported bitter orange marmalade, but any quality brand will work. Green peas and rice flecked with diced red onions would make this a very pretty party dish.

8 skinless, boneless chicken breast halves
   (about 5 ounces each)
   Salt and freshly ground pepper
²/₃ cup orange marmalade
4 tablespoons butter
¹/₄ cup dry white wine
3 tablespoons grated fresh ginger

1. Preheat the broiler. Pound the chicken breasts slightly to flatten evenly. Season with salt and pepper.

2. In a small saucepan, heat the marmalade, butter, wine and ginger over medium-low heat for about 2 minutes, stirring occasionally, until the butter is melted and the marmalade is liquefied. Brush both sides of the chicken with some of the marmalade mixture and place on a broiler pan.

3. Broil about 4 inches from the heat, turning once and basting several times with the marmalade mixture, until the chicken is golden on the outside and white but still moist in the center, 7 to 8 minutes.

8 SERVINGS

BROILED HONEY MUSTARD CHICKEN

Honey mustard is readily available in supermarkets these days, and its sweet-hot flavor lends a rich tang to chicken. This is an elegant and easy dish for entertaining, especially if presented with wild rice pilaf and a spinach salad.

8 skinless, boneless chicken breast halves
  (about 5 ounces each)
  Freshly ground pepper
1/2 cup honey mustard
1/4 cup olive oil
1/4 cup plus 2 tablespoons minced shallots
3 tablespoons chopped fresh thyme leaves or 1 tablespoon dried

1. Preheat the broiler. Pound the chicken breasts to flatten evenly. Season with pepper.

2. In a shallow dish, combine the mustard and oil. Whisk to mix well. Stir in the shallots and thyme. One at a time, coat the chicken breasts on both sides with the mustard mixture and place on a broiler pan.

3. Broil about 4 inches from the heat, turning once and basting with any remaining sauce, until the chicken is golden on the outside and white but still moist in the center, 7 to 8 minutes.

8 SERVINGS

BAKED CHICKEN ITALIANO

Seasoned bread crumbs vary widely in quality. Choose a good brand, then use the crumbs within a few weeks of opening the package to be sure they remain fresh tasting. Serve this with a side dish of linguine or other pasta topped with more of the bottled marinara sauce. Add a green salad for a great family meal.

4 skinless, boneless chicken breast halves
   (about 5 ounces each)
$3/4$ cup dry bread crumbs seasoned with Italian herbs
$1/4$ cup grated Parmesan cheese
$1/4$ teaspoon freshly ground pepper
$1/4$ cup olive oil
1 cup marinara sauce

1. Preheat the oven to 500 degrees F. Pound the chicken slightly to flatten evenly. In a shallow dish, combine the bread crumbs, Parmesan cheese and pepper. Toss to mix.

2. Brush the chicken generously with the oil, then dredge in the bread crumb mixture to coat completely. Place the chicken on a baking sheet.

3. Bake until the chicken is white in the center but still juicy and the coating is golden brown, about 9 minutes. If the crumbs aren't brown enough, place under the broiler for about 1 minute.

4. While the chicken is baking, heat the marinara sauce. Ladle the sauce over the chicken just before serving.

4 SERVINGS

Broiled Peachy Chicken

Broiled fruit is absolutely delicious. This summer recipe is best made with ripe but not soft peaches and good-quality preserves.

4 skinless, boneless chicken breast halves
   Salt and freshly ground pepper
1 medium lemon
$1/3$ cup peach preserves
2 tablespoons butter
2 medium peaches

1. Preheat the broiler. Pound the chicken breasts slightly to flatten evenly. Season generously with salt and pepper. Grate $3/4$ teaspoon of colored zest and squeeze 2 tablespoons of juice from the lemon.

2. In a small nonreactive saucepan, combine the peach preserves, butter, lemon zest and lemon juice. Cook over medium-low heat, stirring occasionally, until the preserves melt, about 2 minutes. Cut the unpeeled peaches into $1/4$-inch-thick slices.

3. Brush both sides of the chicken with some of the preserves mixture and place on a broiler pan. Broil about 4 inches from the heat for 4 minutes. Add the peach slices to the broiler pan. Turn the chicken over and brush both chicken and peaches with more of the preserves.

4. Broil for about 4 minutes longer, turning the chicken and fruit once and basting again, until the chicken is golden outside and white in the center and the peaches are glazed and softened.

4 SERVINGS

ROASTED CHICKEN PRIMAVERA

Lots of other vegetables can be substituted, including broccoli, squash and all colors of peppers. If you can find slim leeks, try them in place of green onions for a delicate taste of spring.

6 skinless, boneless chicken breast halves
   (about 5 ounces each)
2 garlic cloves
1/3 cup extra virgin olive oil
1/2 teaspoon salt
1/2 teaspoon freshly ground pepper
2 bunches of green onions
2 medium yellow bell peppers

1. Preheat the oven to 500 degrees F. Pound the chicken breasts slightly to flatten evenly. Finely chop the garlic and combine in a small bowl with the olive oil, salt and pepper. Trim the green onions but leave them whole. Cut each pepper into 8 wedges.

2. Arrange the chicken and vegetables in a single layer on a large baking sheet. Brush with about half of the seasoned oil. Roast for 4 minutes, then turn chicken and vegetables, brush with remaining oil and roast 4 minutes longer, or until the vegetables are softened and deeply browned at the edges and the chicken is white in the center but still juicy.

3. To serve, arrange the vegetables over and around the chicken.

6 SERVINGS

CHICKEN AND SPAGHETTI PIE

1 pound skinless, boneless chicken breasts
Salt and freshly ground pepper
12 ounces spaghetti
$\frac{1}{3}$ cup grated Parmesan cheese
2 cups bottled spaghetti sauce flavored with basil
2 cups shredded mozzarella cheese (about 8 ounces)

1. Preheat the broiler. Cut the chicken into $\frac{3}{4}$-inch chunks. Place the chicken in a large pot of salted water. Bring to a boil over high heat. Just before the water actually boils, the chicken should be cooked. Remove the chicken with a slotted spoon and set aside.

2. Break the spaghetti in half and add to the same pot of boiling water. Cook until it is tender but still firm, about 8 minutes. Drain the spaghetti and toss it with the Parmesan cheese.

3. Spread the spaghetti in the bottom and slightly up the sides of a 9-by-13-inch baking dish. Set under the broiler about 4 inches from the heat for 1 minute. Spread half of the sauce over the spaghetti, arrange the chicken evenly over the sauce and spread the remaining sauce over the chicken. Sprinkle the shredded mozzarella cheese on top.

4. Broil for about 1 minute, until cheese is melted and bubbly. Cut into squares to serve. Each square should have some of the outer edge or "crust."

6 TO 8 SERVINGS

BROILED TERIYAKI CHICKEN

For a super-easy party, try boiling some whole scallions along with the chicken, then round out the meal with simple steamed rice and a platter of tropical fruits for dessert. These chicken chunks can be skewered before broiling, if you like. This recipe is also wonderful on the grill.

6 skinless, boneless chicken breast halves
   (about 5 ounces each)
   Freshly ground pepper
3 tablespoons Asian sesame oil
3 tablespoons soy sauce
3 tablespoons sweet sherry
3 tablespoons rice wine vinegar

1. Preheat the broiler. Cut chicken into 1½-inch chunks. Season with pepper.

2. In a shallow dish, combine the sesame oil, soy sauce, sherry and vinegar. Stir to mix well. One at a time, dip the chicken pieces to coat evenly, then place them on a broiler pan.

3. Broil about 4 inches from the heat, turning once and basting several times with the sauce, until the chicken is golden on the outside and white but still moist in the center, 7 to 8 minutes.

6 SERVINGS

WORLD'S FASTEST CHICKEN TETRAZZINI

1 pound skinless, boneless chicken breasts
1 pound thin egg noodles
1 pound frozen creamed spinach in a microwave pouch
1 container (15 ounces) ricotta cheese
$1/2$ cup grated Parmesan cheese
$1/4$ teaspoon salt
$1/2$ teaspoon freshly ground pepper

1. Preheat the broiler. Cut the chicken into $3/4$-inch chunks. Place the chicken in a large pot of salted water. Bring to a boil over high heat. Just before the water actually boils, the chicken should be cooked. Remove the chicken with a slotted spoon and set aside. Check to be sure it is white to the center.

2. Add the noodles to the same pot of boiling water. Cook until tender but still firm, about 6 minutes. Drain well.

3. While the chicken and noodles are cooking, cook the spinach in a microwave oven on High for about 2 minutes, or until thawed and hot; place in a large bowl. Add the ricotta cheese, $1/4$ cup plus 2 tablespoons of the Parmesan cheese, the salt and the pepper. Stir until mixed. Add the chicken and pasta and toss to blend.

4. Spread the mixture in a 9-by-13-inch baking dish. Sprinkle the remaining Parmesan cheese over the top. Broil about 1 minute, until bubbly and tinged with gold.

6 TO 8 SERVINGS

6 BARBECUES AND GRILLS

The barbecue grill has been an American fixture for years, with burgers, steaks and ribs the traditional standbys. But these days, because of the new interest in lighter and more adventurous dining, you're as likely to find a lean boneless chicken breast as a piece of red meat on the backyard grill.

Also, it's worth noting that grilling isn't just for summer anymore, either. With instant-on gas-fired units, people who live in the snowy northern climes can savor grilled foods year-round with the push of a button. And if grilling isn't your choice, any of these recipes will take quite nicely to the indoor broiler.

Since cooking heat and times are more variable in outdoor grills, be sure to flatten the raw chicken breasts to an even thickness and then test for doneness before removal from the grill. Also, when basting with a marinade, be sure to stop a minute or two before the chicken is done, so there is no contamination from uncooked sauce.

The recipes in this section range from homespun Vermont Grilled Chicken and Barbecued Chicken Burgers to some really sophisticated fare, such as an Indonesian Chicken Satay and Grilled Chicken with Pineapple Salsa. In short, there is a grilled chicken dish here for all tastes.

ALL-AMERICAN BARBECUED CHICKEN WITH GRILLED ONION

Zip up some bottled barbecue sauce with beer or ale and fresh herbs, then brush it on both the chicken and the sweet onion slices. Start with a premium-quality, thick sauce for best results. Round out this traditional barbecue with cole slaw and French fries or corn on the cob.

> 6 skinless, boneless chicken breast halves
> 1 large sweet onion, such as Vidalia
> 1½ cups thick barbecue sauce
> ¾ cup beer or ale
> 3 tablespoons minced fresh herb of choice, such as oregano or thyme

1. Light a medium-hot fire in a barbecue grill. Pound the chicken breasts slightly to flatten evenly. Cut the onion into 6 slices about ½ inch thick. Combine the barbecue sauce, beer and herbs in a small nonreactive saucepan, then set on the edge of the grill to heat.

2. Brush the chicken and onion slices with some of the sauce. Place the chicken in the center of the grill and the onion slices nearer the edges. Cook, turning the chicken with tongs and the onion with a large spatula, until the chicken and onion are nicely browned on the outside and the chicken is white to the center, about 8 minutes. Brush often with sauce during grilling.

3. Serve the chicken topped with the grilled onion.

6 SERVINGS

CHICKEN BOMBAY

Yogurt makes a tangy coating for grilling chicken. When enhanced with these traditional Indian flavors, the result is particularly nice. For a summer party, a room-temperature curried rice salad tossed with raisins and almonds and sliced ripe tomatoes would be lovely.

2 cups of mint sprigs
8 skinless, boneless chicken breast halves
   (about 5 ounces each)
2 cups plain low-fat or nonfat yogurt
1 cup chopped red onion
4 teaspoons ground coriander

1. Light a medium-hot fire in a barbecue grill. Set aside a few mint sprigs for garnish. Place the remaining mint in a food processor and process in quick pulses, until the mint is chopped; there should be about 1 cup.

2. Pound the chicken breasts slightly to flatten evenly. In a shallow dish, stir together the yogurt, chopped mint, onion and coriander. Add the chicken and turn to coat completely with the sauce.

3. Grill the chicken 4 minutes. Brush with any remaining sauce, turn and grill about 4 minutes longer, or until outside is nicely browned and the inside is white but still moist in the center.

4. Serve garnished with the reserved mint sprigs.

8 SERVINGS

BARBECUED CHICKEN BURGERS

We grind our own chicken here—in a flash in a food processor—to be sure we are using only the light breast meat and no extra fat. If your market sells lean ground chicken breast, by all means save more time by using it. Serve these light burgers with all the traditional condiments and accompaniments you would offer with hamburgers: lettuce and sliced tomatoes, pickles, potato or tortilla chips, ketchup, mustard and mayonnaise.

> 1 pound skinless, boneless chicken breasts
> 1¹/₂ tablespoons vegetable oil
> 1 teaspoon freshly ground pepper
> ¹/₂ teaspoon salt
> 4 slices of Cheddar, Swiss or Monterey Jack cheese
> 4 slices of red onion
> 4 hamburger buns

1. Light a medium-hot fire in a barbecue grill. Cut the chicken into 1-inch chunks, then place in a food processor. Add the oil, pepper and salt and process, pulsing on and off, just until the chicken is ground; do not puree into a paste. Form the ground chicken into 4 patties about ¹/₂ inch thick.

2. On an oiled grill rack, grill the chicken burgers a total of about 8 minutes, turning once or twice, until nicely browned on the outside and white but still moist in the center. About 2 minutes before the burgers are done, top each with a slice of cheese to melt. Serve the burgers and the onion on the buns.

4 SERVINGS

CHICKEN BRUSCHETTA

Good-quality frozen garlic bread is available in supermarkets these days. It will thaw and be ready to use in the time it takes to build the barbecue fire.

1/4 cup extra virgin olive oil
1/4 cup chopped fresh basil, plus fresh basil sprigs for garnish
1/4 teaspoon salt
1/4 teaspoon freshly ground pepper
 2 firm, ripe tomatoes
 1 pound thinly sliced chicken cutlets
 1 loaf (10 to 12 ounces) frozen garlic bread

1. Build a medium-hot fire in a barbecue grill. In a small dish, combine the olive oil, chopped basil, salt and pepper. Cut the tomatoes into 8 thick slices. Brush the chicken and the tomato slices with some of the seasoned oil. Separate the top and bottom halves of the garlic bread.

2. Grill the chicken for 4 minutes. Brush with more oil. Turn the chicken, then add the tomatoes and the garlic bread, cut sides down, to the grill. Grill 4 minutes longer, or until chicken is nicely browned and white but still moist in the center, the garlic bread is toasted and the tomatoes have just begun to soften.

3. To serve, layer the garlic toast with chicken, then the tomato slices. Sprinkle with additional pepper. Garnish with fresh basil leaves if desired.

4 SERVINGS

GRILLED CURRIED CHICKEN

Curry powder is really a distinctive blend of many different spices and is thus a particularly useful ingredient for cooks who want to prepare "exotic" company dishes in a limited time frame. Serve this with chutney and classic Indian *raita*, diced cucumbers mixed with yogurt and with toasted pita or Indian flatbreads.

8 skinless, boneless chicken breast halves
4 garlic cloves
1 large bunch of green onions
2 cups plain low-fat or nonfat yogurt
4 teaspoons curry powder
3/4 teaspoon salt
1/2 teaspoon freshly ground pepper

1. Light a medium-hot fire in a barbecue grill. Pound the chicken breasts slightly to flatten evenly. Chop the garlic. Thinly slice the green onions. Measure out 1 cup sliced green onions; reserve the remainder for garnish.

2. In a shallow dish, combine the yogurt, curry powder, salt, pepper, garlic and 1 cup of sliced green onions. Add the chicken and turn to coat evenly.

3. Grill a total of about 8 minutes, turning and brushing often with the yogurt mixture, until the chicken is nicely browned on the outside and white but still moist in the center. (Stop basting at least 1 minute before removing the food, so that the marinade is fully cooked.) Serve garnished with the remaining sliced green onion.

8 SERVINGS

GRILLED CHICKEN WITH DILLED CUCUMBER AND YOGURT SAUCE

Cucumbers and dill have a natural affinity for each other. Stirred into tangy plain yogurt, the combination is a delightful, nonfat sauce for grilled chicken. Serve with sliced tomatoes and baked potatoes.

4 skinless, boneless chicken breast halves (about 5 ounces each)
$1/2$ teaspoon salt
$1/2$ teaspoon freshly ground pepper
1 cup plain nonfat yogurt
1 medium cucumber, peeled, seeded and diced (about 1 cup)
2 tablespoons minced fresh dill, or 2 teaspoons dried, plus sprigs of fresh dill for garnish

1. Light a medium-hot fire in a barbecue grill. Season the chicken with half each of the salt and the pepper. In a bowl, stir together the yogurt, cucumber, dill and remaining salt and pepper. Let stand at room temperature.

2. On an oiled grill rack, grill the chicken a total of about 8 minutes, turning once, until nicely browned on the outside and white but still moist in the center.

3. Serve the chicken breasts topped with a generous spoonful of the cucumber and yogurt sauce. Garnish with fresh dill sprigs, if you have them.

4 SERVINGS

GRILLED CHICKEN WITH EMERALD HERB BUTTER

Bright green dill, chives and parsley are particularly tasty together, and they are usually easy to find fresh. But feel free to substitute almost any herb that you like here. Almost any pasta salad and a plate of sliced ripe tomatoes would turn this simple summertime dish into a menu well suited to entertaining.

6 skinless, boneless chicken breast halves
3/8 teaspoon salt
3/8 teaspoon freshly ground pepper
4 tablespoons butter, softened
3 tablespoons chopped fresh dill, or 2 teaspoons dried
3 tablespoons snipped chives
3 tablespoons chopped flat-leaf parsley, plus sprigs for garnish

1. Light a medium-hot fire in a barbecue grill. Pound the chicken breasts slightly to flatten evenly. Season the chicken with a little of the salt and pepper.

2. In a small bowl or in a mini food processor, blend together the butter, the dill, chives, parsley and remaining salt and pepper.

3. On an oiled grill rack, grill the chicken for about 8 minutes, turning once or twice until nicely browned and white but still moist in center. To serve, overlap the chicken decoratively on a plate. Top with the herb butter and garnish with parsley sprigs.

6 SERVINGS

GREEK ISLANDS CHICKEN GRILL

1 pound thinly sliced chicken cutlets
  Salt and freshly ground pepper
2 lemons
2 garlic cloves
3 tablespoons extra virgin olive oil
1 teaspoon dried oregano

1. Light a hot fire in a barbecue grill. Season the chicken with salt and pepper. Grate 1 teaspoon of colored zest and squeeze 3 tablespoons of juice from 1 of the lemons. Thinly slice the other lemon. Mince the garlic.

2. In a small nonreactive saucepan, heat the olive oil. Add the garlic and oregano and cook over medium-low heat until the garlic is softened and fragrant, about 1 minute. Remove from the heat and stir in the lemon juice and zest.

3. Dip the chicken into the garlic-lemon mixture to coat completely. Set on the grill and cook for 3 minutes. Brush the lemon slices with the sauce and add to the grill. Grill the chicken and lemon slices an additional 3 minutes, turning and brushing often with the sauce until the chicken and lemon are nicely browned and white in the center. (Stop basting at least 1 minute before removing the food from the grill, so that the marinade is fully cooked.)

4 SERVINGS

HOT AND SPICY BARBECUED CHICKEN

This dish is not for the faint of heart. If you are a bit timid about spicy flavors, simply go a little easier on the hot pepper flakes. Balance the heat with a cool cole slaw and some crusty rolls.

2 garlic cloves
1/4 cup olive oil
1 tablespoon Worcestershire sauce
1 teaspoon crushed dried hot red pepper flakes
1 pound thinly sliced chicken cutlets

1. Light a hot fire in a barbecue grill. Chop the garlic. In a shallow dish, combine the garlic, oil, Worcestershire sauce and hot pepper flakes. Dip the chicken in the sauce to coat completely.

2. Grill the chicken a total of about 6 minutes, turning and brushing often with sauce, until it is nicely browned and white in the center.

4 SERVINGS

INDONESIAN CHICKEN SATAY

Though an authentic satay has many more ingredients and a more complex flavor, this quick and easy version accents the major flavors and tastes terrific. You can use the traditional bamboo skewers, but they need to be soaked in warm water for at least 30 minutes first to prevent burning. Plain white or aromatic basmati rice and a cooling cucumber salad would be good with the satay.

1 pound skinless, boneless chicken breasts
2 large garlic cloves
6 tablespoons peanut butter
3 tablespoons soy sauce
½ teaspoon crushed dried hot red pepper flakes

1. Light a medium-hot fire in a barbecue grill. Cut the chicken into 1-inch cubes. Mince the garlic. In a medium bowl, whisk together the peanut butter, soy sauce, pepper flakes, garlic and 3 tablespoons hot water until the mixture is blended.

2. Add the chicken to the bowl and stir to coat all pieces thoroughly with the peanut butter mixture. Thread the chicken onto metal or water-soaked bamboo skewers.

3. Grill for 4 minutes. Baste the chicken with any additional sauce, turn the skewers over and grill 4 minutes longer, or until the chicken is nicely browned and white in the center.

4 SERVINGS

JAMAICAN JERK CHICKEN

Commercial jerk seasoning mix is increasingly available in the spice sections of supermarkets. If you can find it, use it in place of the allspice and cayenne. Complement this spicy Jamaican specialty with a classic "peas 'n rice" dish (seasoned rice cooked with black or red beans) and a salad of tropical fruits.

2 limes
3 tablespoons vegetable oil
1 teaspoon ground allspice
$1/2$ teaspoon cayenne pepper
1 pound thinly sliced chicken cutlets

1. Light a hot fire in a barbecue grill. Grate 1 teaspoon of colored zest and squeeze 3 tablespoons of juice from $1^{1/2}$ of the limes. Thinly slice the remaining lime half.

2. In a shallow dish, stir together the oil, allspice, cayenne, lime zest and lime juice. Add the chicken and turn to coat completely.

3. Grill the chicken for 5 or 6 minutes, turning 2 or 3 times and brushing with the remaining oil mixture until the chicken is nicely browned and white in the center. (Stop basting at least 1 minute before removing the food, so that the marinade is fully cooked.) Serve garnished with the lime slices.

4 SERVINGS

GRILLED CHICKEN WITH LEMON AND FENNEL BUTTER

Pernod is an anise-based liqueur, in the same flavor family as fennel seeds. Together with the lightness of lemon, the result is a potent seasoned butter that is memorable on grilled chicken.

```
 1 pound thinly sliced chicken cutlets
   Salt and freshly ground pepper
 2 lemons
2½ tablespoons butter, softened
 1 tablespoon Pernod
 1 teaspoon fennel seeds
```

1. Light a medium-hot fire in a barbecue grill. Season the chicken generously with salt and pepper. Grate 2 teaspoons of the colored zest and squeeze 1 tablespoon of juice from 1½ lemons. Thinly slice the remaining lemon half.

2. In a small bowl or in a mini food processor, combine the butter, Pernod, fennel seeds, lemon zest, lemon juice and a pinch each of salt and pepper. Blend very well. Let stand at room temperature while you cook the chicken.

3. On an oiled grill rack, grill the chicken for a total of about 6 minutes, turning once or twice, until nicely browned and white in the center. To serve, arrange the chicken in overlapping slices on a plate and top with some of the lemon and fennel butter. Garnish with the lemon slices.

4 SERVINGS

BLACKENED CHICKEN WITH LEMON MAYONNAISE

Some commercial "blackened" seasonings, readily found in the spice section of the market, are much spicier and peppery than others, so try a few to see which you prefer. The fiery taste of the chicken is nicely soothed by the creamy lemon-scented mayonnaise sauce. Baked potato and broccoli are pleasing accompaniments.

  3 tablespoons vegetable oil
  1 tablespoon "blackened" spice seasoning blend
  1 pound thinly sliced chicken cutlets
  1 medium lemon
½ cup mayonnaise

1. Light a hot fire in a barbecue grill. In a shallow dish, stir together the oil and "blackened" seasonings. Add the chicken and turn to coat both sides with the mixture.

2. Grate 2 teaspoons of colored zest and squeeze 1 tablespoon of juice from the lemon. In a small bowl, stir together the lemon zest, lemon juice and mayonnaise. Let stand at room temperature while you cook the chicken.

3. Grill the chicken a total of about 5 minutes, until it is nicely browned outside and white in the center. Spoon the lemon mayonnaise over the chicken and serve.

4 SERVINGS

GRILLED LEMON TARRAGON CHICKEN

Fresh tarragon is really very special, so it is worth growing or buying. Dried tarragon is fine, especially if you first rub it between your finger and thumb to warm it and bring out the natural oils. This rather sophisticated main course is excellent with a simple pasta salad and steamed asparagus.

1 large lemon
1 large garlic clove
1/4 cup olive oil
2 tablespoons minced fresh tarragon, or 1 1/2 teaspoons dried
  tarragon, plus additional fresh tarragon for garnish
  Salt and freshly ground pepper
1 pound thinly sliced chicken cutlets

1. Light a medium-hot fire in a barbecue grill. Grate the colored zest and squeeze 3 tablespoons of juice from the lemon. Chop the garlic.

2. In a shallow dish, combine the oil, tarragon, lemon zest, lemon juice and garlic. Stir to mix well. Season generously with salt and pepper. Add the chicken to the dish and turn to coat evenly with the oil mixture.

3. Grill the chicken for a total of about 6 minutes, or until nicely browned on the outside and white in the center. Serve garnished with fresh tarragon sprigs if you have them.

4 SERVINGS

CHICKEN AND MELON KEBABS

It may sound surprising, but cantaloupe and honeydew melon taste wonderful when lightly grilled. These days, you can save even more time by buying these fruits already cut in chunks at the supermarket salad bar.

1 pound skinless, boneless chicken breasts
1 cantaloupe or honeydew melon (or 3 cups melon cubes)
3 tablespoons lemon juice
2 tablespoons vegetable oil
1 tablespoon grated fresh ginger
1/4 teaspoon salt
1/4 teaspoon freshly ground pepper

1. Light a medium-hot fire in a barbecue grill. Cut the chicken into 1-inch cubes. Cut the melon into 1½-inch slices. Scrape out seeds and cut off peel. Cut melon crosswise into 1½-inch cubes.

2. In a shallow dish, combine the lemon juice, oil, ginger, salt and pepper. Add the chicken and melon and stir and toss gently to coat both with the sauce.

3. Thread the chicken and melon onto 4 large skewers, alternating the ingredients. Grill for about 8 minutes, turning and brushing often with the sauce remaining in the bowl, until the chicken and melon are nicely browned and the chicken is white but still moist in center. (Stop basting at least 1 minute before removing the food from the grill, so that the marinade is fully cooked.)

4 SERVINGS

GRILLED MOLASSES AND MUSTARD CHICKEN

This tangy chicken tastes like sophisticated barbecue sauce without the tomatoes. Sweet molasses and spicy mustard are a great combination stemming from our colonial days, and the rum is a natural to tie it all together. Good accompaniments for an easy party are potato salad and corn on the cob.

8 skinless, boneless chicken breast halves
   (about 5 ounces each)
   Salt and freshly ground pepper
6 tablespoons molasses
6 tablespoons vegetable oil
1/4 cup dark rum
4 teaspoons dry mustard

1. Light a medium-hot fire in a barbecue grill. Pound the chicken breasts slightly to flatten evenly. Season with salt and pepper. In a shallow dish, blend together the molasses, oil, rum and mustard, whisking until the mustard is dissolved. Add the chicken breasts and turn to coat with the molasses mixture.

2. Grill the chicken a total of about 8 minutes, turning and brushing with the molasses mixture several times, until the chicken is nicely browned on the outside and white but still moist in the center. (Stop basting at least 1 minute before removing the food, so that the marinade is fully cooked.)

8 SERVINGS

GRILLED CHICKEN WITH
OLIVE AND MARJORAM BUTTER

Regular canned ripe olives will work here, but we recommend that you try some of the many varieties of wonderful olives sold at most supermarket deli counters these days. Kalamata and Mediterranean oil-cured are only a few of the types available. Some markets even sell a mix of tasty olives that would work beautifully in this delicious seasoned butter.

1/4 cup black olives
2 1/2 tablespoons butter, softened
1/4 cup finely chopped red onion
2 teaspoons chopped fresh marjoram, or 1/2 teaspoon dried, plus fresh sprigs for garnish
1/4 teaspoon freshly ground black pepper
1 pound thinly sliced chicken cutlets

1. Build a medium-hot fire in a barbecue grill. If the olives have pits, cut the olive away from the pit. Coarsely chop the olives. In a small bowl, blend together the butter, chopped olives, red onion, marjoram and pepper.

2. On an oiled grill rack, grill the chicken a total of about 6 minutes, turning once or twice, until nicely browned outside and white in the center. To serve, overlap the chicken pieces on a plate and top with some of the softened olive butter. Garnish with fresh marjoram sprigs if you have them.

4 SERVINGS

ORANGE AND HONEY GRILLED CHICKEN

Our friend Betty introduced us to this great grill recipe several years ago. We quickly incorporated it into our repertoire. Betty likes to serve it with corn muffins and a big tossed salad.

4 skinless, boneless chicken breast halves
2 oranges
2 tablespoons vegetable oil
2 tablespoons honey
2 tablespoons soy sauce
$1/4$ teaspoon freshly ground pepper

1. Light a medium-hot fire in a barbecue grill. Pound the chicken breasts slightly to flatten evenly. Squeeze 3 tablespoons juice from 1 orange. Cut the remaining orange into $1/4$-inch slices.

2. In a shallow bowl, whisk together the orange juice, orange zest, oil, honey, soy sauce and pepper. Dip the chicken into the sauce to coat completely.

3. Grill the chicken for 4 minutes, turning once and brushing with sauce. Brush the orange slices with some of the sauce and place on the grill. Grill the chicken and the oranges for an additional 4 minutes, turning and brushing with sauce until the chicken and oranges are nicely browned and the chicken is white but still moist in center. (Stop basting at least 1 minute before removing the food, so that the marinade is fully cooked.)

4 SERVINGS

GRILLED CHICKEN WITH PESTO BUTTER

The classic Italian flavor combination of basil and Parmesan Cheese has myriad uses. Make the pesto butter in quantity, form into a log and store for up to a month in the freezer. Then slice off as much as needed to make garlic bread, top a grilled piece of fish or a steak or toss with angel hair pasta for a fabulous side dish.

      1 pound thinly sliced chicken cutlets
        Salt and freshly ground pepper
      2 garlic cloves
    2½ tablespoons butter, softened
      ¼ cup chopped fresh basil, plus whole leaves for garnish
      2 tablespoons grated Parmesan cheese

1. Light a medium-hot fire in a barbecue grill. Season the chicken with salt and pepper. Mince the garlic.

2. In a small bowl or mini food processor, blend together the butter, chopped basil, Parmesan cheese, garlic and a generous sprinkling of pepper. (The seasoned butter can be prepared a day ahead and refrigerated. Let return to room temperature before using.)

3. On an oiled grill rack, grill the chicken for a total of about 6 minutes, turning once or twice, until nicely browned and white in the center. To serve, overlap the chicken decoratively on a plate. Top with the seasoned butter and garnish with the basil leaves.

4 SERVINGS

GRILLED CHICKEN WITH PINEAPPLE SALSA

Many supermarkets sell cut-up pineapple cubes. If they are very sweet and juicy, you can chop and use them in place of canned.

4 skinless, boneless chicken breast halves
  Salt and freshly ground pepper
1/2 medium red bell pepper
 1 cup canned crushed pineapple in juice
1/2 cup plus 1 tablespoon thinly sliced green onions
 2 tablespoons chopped fresh cilantro or parsley, plus sprigs for garnish

1. Light a medium-hot fire in a barbecue grill. Pound the chicken breasts gently to flatten evenly. Season lightly with salt and pepper. Finely dice the red pepper.

2. In a medium bowl, stir together the pineapple with its juice, 1/2 cup sliced green onions, the red pepper and the chopped cilantro. Season with salt and generously with pepper to taste. Let stand at room temperature while you cook the chicken.

3. On an oiled grill rack, grill the chicken a total of about 8 minutes, turning 2 to 3 times, until the chicken is nicely browned on the outside and white but still moist in the center.

4. Serve the chicken topped with a generous spoonful of pineapple salsa. Garnish with the remaining green onion slices and sprigs of cilantro.

4 SERVINGS

GRILLED CHICKEN WITH ROASTED PEPPER AND CAPER COMPOTE

Roasted red peppers in a jar are one of our favorite convenience products. Enlivened with the crunch of sweet onion and the saltiness of capers, this compote is good on fish or pasta, too.

6 skinless, boneless chicken breast halves
    (about 5 ounces each)
    Freshly ground pepper
1 jar (7½ ounces) drained roasted red peppers
3 tablespoons olive oil
¾ cup chopped sweet onion
3 tablespoons tiny (nonpareil) capers plus 1½ teaspoons
    brine from capers

1. Light a medium-hot fire in a barbecue grill. Pound the chicken breasts slightly to flatten evenly. Season generously with pepper. Coarsely chop or thinly slice the roasted peppers. In a small bowl, stir together the olive oil, roasted peppers, onion, capers and caper brine. Season with pepper. Let stand at room temperature while you cook the chicken.

2. On an oiled grill rack, grill the chicken a total of about 8 minutes, turning several times, until the chicken is nicely browned on the outside and white but still moist in the center.

3. To serve, partially slice the chicken and fan out the slices on a plate. Spoon the compote over the chicken.

6 SERVINGS

ROMAN CHICKEN BROCHETTES

For great flavor with very few ingredients, the trick here is to buy a good-quality bottled Italian vinaigrette salad dressing. Beyond that, you can substitute red and green peppers or summer squash for those listed in the recipe. Let your market (or garden) availability be the guide for this summertime grill.

1 pound skinless, boneless chicken breasts
1 large yellow bell pepper
1 medium zucchini
3/4 cup bottled Italian vinaigrette salad dressing
8 cherry tomatoes
Freshly ground black pepper

1. Light a medium-hot fire in a barbecue grill. Cut the chicken into 1-inch cubes. Cut the bell pepper and zucchini into 1½-inch pieces.

2. Pour the Italian dressing into a shallow dish. Add the chicken, pepper, zucchini and cherry tomatoes and toss to coat thoroughly. Thread the chicken and vegetables onto each of 4 long metal skewers, alternating the ingredients and beginning and ending with the cherry tomatoes. (Do not crowd the chicken pieces.) Season generously with black pepper.

3. Grill for 4 minutes. Brush with any remaining Italian dressing in the bowl, turn the skewers over and grill about 4 minutes longer, until the chicken and vegetables are nicely browned and the chicken is white but still moist in the center.

4 SERVINGS

GRILLED CHICKEN WITH SALSA FRESCA

Bottled salsas are fine, but nothing beats the "fresca" taste of ripe tomatoes and fresh cilantro. This is sure to become one of your summertime favorites, served with corn on the cob and warmed flour tortillas.

    1 pound thinly sliced chicken cutlets
      Salt and freshly ground pepper
 3/4 pound ripe, firm tomatoes
    2 teaspoons pickled jalapeño peppers, plus 2 teaspoons
      pickling juice
2 1/2 tablespoons corn oil
  1/2 cup chopped fresh cilantro, plus sprigs for garnish

1. Light a medium-hot fire in a barbecue grill. Season the chicken lightly with salt and pepper. Seed and coarsely chop the tomatoes. Mince the jalapeño peppers.

2. In a bowl, stir together the oil, tomatoes, minced jalapeños, reserved juice and the chopped cilantro. Let stand at room temperature while you cook the chicken.

3. On an oiled grill rack, grill the chicken a total of about 6 minutes, turning once, until it is nicely browned and cooked through. Spoon the salsa over the chicken. Garnish with cilantro sprigs and serve.

4 SERVINGS

GRILLED CHICKEN AND SUMMER VEGETABLE PLATTER

Round out this pretty main course with nothing more than lots of crusty garlic bread. If you have a large grill, the recipe can easily be doubled and still stay within the time frame!

1 medium red bell pepper
1 small yellow crookneck squash
1 Japanese eggplant or 1 small regular eggplant
$\frac{1}{2}$ pound thinly sliced chicken cutlets
    Salt and freshly ground pepper
6 tablespoons bottled Italian vinaigrette salad dressing

1. Light a medium-hot fire in a barbecue grill. Cut the pepper into 1-inch slices. Cut the squash and eggplant into long diagonal slices, each about $\frac{1}{4}$ inch thick. Season the vegetables and the chicken lightly with salt and generously with pepper. Pour the salad dressing into a shallow dish. Add the chicken and vegetables and turn to coat completely.

2. Place the chicken in the center of the grill and the vegetables around it. Grill a total of about 6 minutes, turning and brushing with the remaining Italian dressing, until the chicken and vegetables are nicely browned and cooked through. (Stop basting at least 1 minute before removing the food from the grill, so that the marinade is fully cooked.)

2 SERVINGS

VERMONT GRILLED CHICKEN

Maple syrup has myriad uses beyond a pancake topper. It lends a wonderful, slightly woodsy flavor to grilled foods. We especially like this sauce combination and serve it often during our New England summers.

1 pound thinly sliced chicken cutlets
   Salt and freshly ground pepper
¼ cup bottled chili sauce
2 tablespoons vegetable oil
3 tablespoons maple syrup
1 tablespoon cider vinegar

1. Light a hot fire in a barbecue grill. Season the chicken with salt and pepper.

2. In a shallow dish, blend together the chili sauce, oil, maple syrup and vinegar. Dip the chicken in the sauce to coat completely.

3. Grill the chicken for a total of about 6 minutes, turning and brushing often with the sauce, until the chicken is nicely browned and cooked through. (Stop basting at least 1 minute before removing the food from the grill, so that the marinade is fully cooked.)

4 SERVINGS

7 Hot and Cold Salads

These days, salads are big business. Practically every supermarket of any size anywhere has at least tripled its fresh produce department in the last ten years. Certainly, it is partly the new awareness that fruits and vegetables are very, very good for us that has prompted the change. It is also the increased availability of exotic delicacies and out-of-season fruits from places where winter is reversed. But we think that the biggest reason is that, after decades of mushy green beans and syrupy canned pineapple, we have discovered that fine-quality fresh produce is a deliciously different breed.

So we have a particularly good time perusing the produce section of the market, especially the salad bar, where so many fruits and vegetables are already trimmed, cut and at the ready for streamlined recipe preparation by the 5 in 10 cook. We also tasted some excellent prepared salad dressings (some of them fat free), especially premium labels found in the produce section. For those of us trying to reduce fat intake—and who isn't?—we also found that nationally available low-fat mayonnaise is really quite good, and that low-fat yogurt can be a fine substitute for sour cream in salads. While many of these recipes cook the chicken in oil, note that the oil doubles as the salad dressing.

For salads that call for cooked chicken use leftover chicken or opt for pre-cooked from your supermarket deli.

Chicken Antipasto

An antipasto is, by definition, served before the pasta course. This salad can indeed be offered as a first course, but it is plenty good as a main course at lunch or for a light supper. To save even more time, if you buy the chicken and smoked mozzarella at a deli counter, have it thinly sliced for you.

3/4 pound cooked skinless, boneless chicken breast
6 ounces smoked mozzarella cheese
1 jar (7 1/2 ounces) roasted red peppers
2 jars (6 ounces each) marinated artichokes
2 tablespoons balsamic vinegar
Freshly ground pepper

1. Thinly slice the chicken. Thinly slice or cube the mozzarella. Drain the roasted peppers and cut into 1/2-inch-wide strips. Drain the artichokes, but reserve 1/4 cup of the marinade.

2. To assemble the antipasto, arrange the chicken, cheese, roasted peppers and artichokes on each of 4 plates or on a large platter. Sprinkle the vinegar and reserved artichoke marinade over the salad. Sprinkle a generous grinding of black pepper over the entire antipasto.

4 Servings

AVOCADOS STUFFED WITH CHICKEN SALAD

We prefer dark, rough-skinned Hass avocados for their rich flavor, but the shiny, paler-skinned ones are fine, too. Just be sure they are ripe enough to yield gently to pressure. If hard, leave them to ripen at room temperature. Avocados should not be refrigerated.

3/4 pound cooked skinless, boneless chicken breast
  2 large celery ribs
  2 limes
  1 cup regular or low-fat mayonnaise
    Salt and freshly ground pepper
  2 ripe avocados

1. Cut the chicken into 1/2-inch pieces. Finely chop the celery. Squeeze the juice from 1 1/2 limes. Cut 4 thin slices from the remaining lime half.

2. In a medium mixing bowl, stir together the mayonnaise and lime juice. Add the chicken and celery and stir to mix. Season with salt and pepper to taste.

3. Cut the avocados in half and remove the pits. Fill with the chicken salad, mounding it up in the center, and serve.

4 SERVINGS

BARBECUED CHICKEN SALAD

This recipe uses the convenience of store-bought barbecued chicken. Of course, you can use your own leftover barbecued chicken—or any cooked chicken at all, for that matter. Bottled barbecue sauces vary enormously in quality, so choose a premium brand that you know and like. Shredded iceberg lettuce would provide a cooling foil to this zesty salad.

4 barbecued chicken breasts (about 1½ pounds total)
2 large celery ribs
1 can (11 ounces) corn kernels
¾ cup regular or low-fat mayonnaise
¼ cup premium-quality hickory-smoke barbecue sauce

1. Remove the chicken from the bone, and tear or cut it into ½- to ¾-inch pieces. Thinly slice the celery. Drain the corn.

2. In a medium bowl, stir together the mayonnaise and the barbecue sauce. Add the chicken, celery and corn. Stir to mix. Serve at room temperature or slightly chilled.

4 SERVINGS

BUFFALO CHICKEN SALAD

This is a main-dish salad adaptation of the chicken wing appetizer made famous in Buffalo, New York. Alone, the chicken is searingly hot; but with the lettuce and blue cheese, the pepper is tamed.

> 1 pound skinless, boneless chicken breasts
> Salt
> 1/2 to 3/4 teaspoon cayenne pepper, to taste
> 1 head of iceberg lettuce
> 3 tablespoons vegetable oil
> 1/2 cup good-quality bottled blue cheese salad dressing, regular or low-fat

1. Cut the chicken into 1-inch cubes. Season with salt and the cayenne pepper. Shred the lettuce by slicing it thinly with a large sharp knife. Place in a large bowl.

2. Heat the oil in a large frying pan, preferably nonstick. Add the chicken and sauté over medium-high heat, stirring often, until the chicken is browned on the outside and white but still juicy in the center, about 6 minutes. Use a slotted spoon to remove the chicken from the frying pan.

3. To serve, drizzle the pan juices over the shredded lettuce and toss to mix. Divide the lettuce among 4 plates. Spoon the chicken over the lettuce and top with the blue cheese dressing.

4 SERVINGS

CAESAR CHICKEN SALAD

The original Caesar salad is attributed to a bartender in Tijuana, Mexico. We have taken several liberties, including the addition of chicken (of course) and the omission of a coddled egg in the dressing. When choosing croutons, try to find either "Caesar"-flavored or cheese and garlic.

1 head of romaine lettuce
1 pound skinless, boneless chicken breasts
  Salt and freshly ground pepper
5 tablespoons extra virgin olive oil
1/4 cup balsamic vinegar
1 cup seasoned bread croutons

1. Tear the lettuce into bite-size pieces and place in a salad bowl. Cut the chicken into strips about 1½ inches long and ½ inch wide. Season with salt and pepper.

2. Heat the oil in a large frying pan over medium heat. Add the chicken and cook until golden brown on the outside and white but still juicy in the center, 5 to 7 minutes. Use a slotted spoon or tongs to remove the chicken from the frying pan. Reduce the heat to medium-low and add the vinegar to the pan. Cook, stirring up browned bits on the bottom of the pan, for 30 seconds.

3. Pour the pan vinaigrette over the romaine and toss to combine. Taste and season lightly with salt and generously with pepper. Add the chicken and croutons and toss again. Spoon the warm salad onto 4 serving plates.

4 SERVINGS

CAJUN CHICKEN SALAD

Use commercial Cajun "blackened" seasoning for the spiciness of this salad. The iceberg lettuce balances the "heat" of the coated chicken. You can shred it yourself or buy it already prepared at the supermarket salad bar. Serve this main-course salad with biscuits and a side dish of parslied rice.

1 pound skinless, boneless chicken breasts
1 tablespoon Cajun "blackened" spice seasoning
6 cups shredded or thinly sliced iceberg lettuce
1/3 cup vegetable oil
3 tablespoons red wine vinegar
  Salt and freshly ground pepper

1. Cut the chicken into strips about 1½ inches long and ½ inch wide. Toss with the "blackened" seasoning to coat the chicken. Divide the lettuce among 4 serving plates.

2. Heat the oil in a large frying pan over medium-high heat. Add the chicken and cook until richly browned on the outside and white but still juicy in the center, 5 to 7 minutes. Reduce the heat to low and add the vinegar to the pan. Cook, stirring, for 30 seconds. Season with salt and pepper to taste.

3. To serve, spoon the chicken and pan vinaigrette over the lettuce.

4 SERVINGS

CANTALOUPE AND
CHUTNEY CHICKEN SALAD

You can either buy a whole cantaloupe or purchase about 1½ cups of mixed melon (no watermelon) balls from the salad bar at the supermarket.

³/₄ pound cooked skinless, boneless chicken breast
 1 small cantaloupe
 2 large celery ribs
¹/₃ cup mango chutney
³/₄ cup regular or low-fat mayonnaise
  Salt and freshly ground pepper

1. Cut the chicken into ½- to ¾-inch pieces. Use a melon baller to make about 1½ cups balls, or cut the melon into small pieces with a knife. Thinly slice the celery. If the chutney has large pieces, chop them before using.

2. In a medium mixing bowl, stir together the mayonnaise and chutney. Add the chicken, melon and celery. Stir to mix. Season with salt and pepper to taste.

4 SERVINGS

STREAMLINED COBB SALAD

This is a classic California chicken salad in which many ingredients are cut into small pieces and arranged decoratively in rows on a plate, but in 5 in 10 fashion, we have pared down both the ingredient list and the preparation time. Accompany with crusty San Francisco-style sourdough bread.

 8 slices of bacon
³/₄ pound cooked skinless, boneless chicken breast
 1 small head of iceberg lettuce
¹/₂ pound plum tomatoes
    Freshly ground pepper
³/₄ cup bottled chunky blue cheese salad dressing

1. Cook the bacon in a frying pan over medium heat or in a microwave oven on High until crisp, 3 to 5 minutes. Drain on paper towels, then coarsely crumble the bacon.

2. Cut the chicken into ¹/₂-inch pieces. Use a sharp knife to thinly slice the head of lettuce or shred in a food processor. Seed the tomatoes, then coarsely chop them.

3. On each serving plate, make a bed of the shredded lettuce. Arrange the tomatoes in a row down the middle of the plates, then make a row of the chicken on the left and the bacon on the right. Season the salads with a grinding of pepper. Spoon about half of the blue cheese dressing across the rows. Pass the remainder at the table.

4 SERVINGS

CURRIED CHICKEN AND PEAR SALAD

Accompanied by a bowl of chutney and some nutty muffins, this salad is a great party buffet dish. Serve on a bed of lettuce. Red Bartlett pears, if they are in season, would lend a lovely color to the salad.

1½ pounds cooked skinless, boneless chicken breast
  4 medium, ripe but firm pears, preferably Red Bartlett
  2 cups regular or low-fat mayonnaise
  2 teaspoons curry powder
 ⅓ cup raisins
    Salt and freshly ground pepper

1. Cut the chicken into ½- to ¾-inch cubes. Cut the unpeeled pears into ½-inch dice.

2. In a medium mixing bowl, stir together the mayonnaise and curry powder until blended. Add the chicken, pears and raisins. Season with salt and pepper to taste and stir again.

8 SERVINGS

DILLED CHICKEN SALAD

Next to parsley, dill seems to be the most common fresh herb
found in supermarkets. It is infinitely superior to dried dill, both in
color and in flavor. This verdant chicken salad looks very pretty
served on a bed of red leaf lettuce surrounded by sliced tomatoes.
A basket of crusty rolls adds texture to the meal.

12 ounces cooked skinless, boneless chicken breast
  1 large bunch of green onions
  1 can (8 ounces) sliced water chestnuts
  1 cup regular or low-fat mayonnaise
$1/3$ cup chopped fresh dill, plus sprigs for garnish
    Salt and freshly ground pepper

1. Cut the chicken into $1/2$- to $3/4$-inch pieces. Thinly slice the green
onions. Drain water chestnuts; rinse and drain well.

2. In a medium mixing bowl, stir together the mayonnaise,
chicken, green onions, water chestnuts and chopped dill. Season
with salt and pepper to taste.

3. Serve garnished with dill sprigs.

3 TO 4 SERVINGS

CHICKEN AND FUSILLI SALAD

Premium-quality Italian salad dressings with Parmesan cheese in them abound on market shelves today. Because of its vinaigrette base, this salad is great for picnics and buffets. Serve with sesame-seeded bread sticks.

  8 ounces fusilli or rotelle pasta
1½ pounds ripe tomatoes
  2 medium green bell peppers
  1 pound skinless, boneless chicken breasts
  1 cup bottled Italian vinaigrette dressing with Parmesan cheese
     Salt and freshly ground pepper

1. Cook the pasta in a large pot of boiling, salted water until tender but still firm, 8 to 10 minutes. Drain into a colander.

2. While the pasta is cooking, seed the tomatoes and cut them into ³/₄-inch chunks. Cut the bell peppers into the same size pieces. Place in a large mixing bowl. Cut the chicken into ¹/₂- to ³/₄-inch pieces.

3. In a large nonreactive frying pan, heat ¹/₂ cup of the Italian dressing. Over medium heat, add the chicken and cook, stirring often, until the chicken is lightly browned on the outside and white but still juicy in the center, 5 to 7 minutes.

4. Pour the chicken and pan juices into the mixing bowl with the vegetables. Add the hot pasta and the remaining ¹/₂ cup Italian dressing and toss to coat. Season with salt and pepper to taste.

4 SERVINGS

GREEK CHICKEN SALAD

Greek salads can be embellished with all sorts of condiments such as black olives, red onion, cucumber and bell peppers. This streamlined version is zesty and full-flavored, and goes well with a basket of warmed pita breads for a light and summery main course when tomatoes are at their peak.

1¼ pounds cooked skinless, boneless chicken breast
   3 medium, ripe and meaty tomatoes (about 12 ounces total)
   1 cup crumbled feta cheese (about 4 ounces)
   1 cup bottled olive oil vinaigrette salad dressing
   1 large head of romaine lettuce
   Freshly ground pepper

1. Cut the chicken into ½- to ¾-inch pieces. Core and seed the tomatoes, then cut into ½-inch dice. In a medium mixing bowl, toss together the chicken, tomatoes, feta cheese and vinaigrette.

2. To serve, separate the romaine lettuce into leaves. Arrange 2 or 3 leaves on each plate. Spoon the chicken salad onto the lettuce. Season generously with pepper.

6 SERVINGS

HAWAIIAN CHICKEN SALAD

Macadamia nuts enrich this salad to make it very special indeed. Accompany with flatbreads or pita wedges to make a meal that will almost transport you to the islands, at least for one meal.

3/4 pound cooked skinless, boneless chicken breast
1/2 medium, sweet onion, such as Maui or Spanish
1/2 cup macadamia nuts
1 can (8 ounces) pineapple tidbits in unsweetened juice
3/4 cup regular or low-fat mayonnaise
Salt and freshly ground pepper

1. Cut the chicken into 1/2- to 3/4-inch pieces. Coarsely chop the onion. Cut the macadamia nuts in half. Drain the pineapple, reserving 2 tablespoons of the juice.

2. In a medium mixing bowl, stir together the mayonnaise and reserved pineapple juice. Add the chicken, onion, macadamia nuts and pineapple. Stir to blend. Season with salt and pepper to taste. (If the nuts are salted, no additional salt will probably be needed.)

4 SERVINGS

HOT AND SOUR CHICKEN SALAD

Hot chili oil and rice wine vinegar are readily available at most supermarkets in the Asian food section. Tame the heat of this very spicy salad with crisp rice cakes or rice crackers. We would end this light meal with lemon frozen yogurt, perhaps with some candied ginger sprinkled on top.

1 small head of Chinese (napa) cabbage
1 pound skinless, boneless chicken breasts
1/2 teaspoon salt
1 large bunch of green onions
1 to 2 tablespoons Chinese hot chili oil, to taste
3 tablespoons rice wine vinegar

1. Thinly slice the Chinese cabbage across the grain; there should be 5 to 6 cups. Place in a large mixing bowl. Cut the chicken into strips about 1½ inches long and ¼ inch wide. Season with the salt. Thinly slice the green onions.

2. Heat the chili oil in a large frying pan. Add the chicken and cook over medium-high heat, stirring often, until white but still moist in center, about 3 minutes. Reduce the heat to low and add the vinegar to the pan. Cook, stirring for 30 seconds, then add the green onions and cook for 20 seconds.

3. To serve, spoon the chicken, green onions and pan vinaigrette over the cabbage and toss to mix well.

4 SERVINGS

LEMON-SCALLION CHICKEN SALAD IN RADICCHIO CUPS

Scallions are green onions, but here the fancier name seems right with such a special salad. Radicchio is that new, rather pricey ruby red tiny head of bitter lettuce that you see in markets. However, a very little goes a long way, so rest assured it won't cost as much as you think. And the beauty it lends as an accent for salads is worth every penny.

3/4 pound cooked skinless boneless chicken breast
1 large bunch of green onions
2 medium lemons
1 cup regular or low-fat mayonnaise
   Salt and freshly ground pepper
1 head of radicchio

1. Cut the chicken into 1/2- to 3/4-inch pieces. Thinly slice the green onions. Grate 1 1/2 teaspoons of zest and squeeze 2 tablespoons of juice from 1 1/2 lemons. Cut 4 thin slices from the remaining lemon half.

2. In a medium mixing bowl, stir together the mayonnaise, lemon juice and lemon zest. Add the chicken and green onions and stir to mix. Season lightly with salt and generously with pepper.

3. To serve, separate the radicchio into leaves. Arrange 3 leaves on each of 4 plates to form "cups." Spoon the salad onto the radicchio. Garnish each portion with a lemon slice.

4 SERVINGS

LIGHT AND BRIGHT CHICKEN AND SWEET ONION SALAD

This fat-free salad is rich with bright colors and sprightly flavors. If you're counting calories, rice cakes make a pleasingly crunchy accompaniment, and you can end the meal with a fruity sorbet.

3/4 pound cooked skinless, boneless chicken breast
  1 medium, sweet onion
  1 large red bell pepper
  2 cups fresh alfalfa or bean sprouts
    Freshly ground pepper
1/2 cup fat-free vinaigrette

1. Thinly slice the chicken (or purchase it thinly sliced). Cut the onion in half and thinly slice. Cut the bell pepper into thin strips.

2. To assemble the salad, spread the sprouts on each of 4 serving plates or on a large platter. Arrange the chicken slices slightly overlapping on the sprouts. Season generously with pepper. Scatter the onion and red pepper slices over the chicken. Drizzle the vinaigrette over the salad.

4 SERVINGS

MINTED COUSCOUS CHICKEN SALAD

Couscous is a tiny pasta from Morocco that can be a stand-in for rice in side dishes or in this wonderful salad. It cooks in almost no time, but has a lovely nutty flavor and unique character. Look for couscous in the rice section of your supermarket. For an informal party, serve this exotic salad on a bed of romaine lettuce, wedges of feta sprinkled with oregano, Greek olives and a basket of toasted pita breads drizzled with a bit of olive oil.

1¼ pounds cooked skinless, boneless chicken breasts
1 medium cucumber
1 cup loosely packed fresh mint
1½ cups instant couscous
¾ teaspoon salt
¾ cup bottled Italian olive oil vinaigrette

1. Cut the chicken into ½-inch dice. Peel the cucumber. Cut in half and scoop out the seeds. Cut the cucumber into ¼- to ⅜-inch dice. Reserve a few sprigs of mint for garnish. Chop the rest (in a food processor to save time); there should be about ½ cup.

2. Bring 2¼ cups of water to a boil. Add the couscous and salt, cover the pan and remove from the heat. Let stand 5 minutes, then turn the couscous into a medium mixing bowl and fluff it with a fork.

3. Add the chicken, cucumber, chopped mint and vinaigrette to the couscous. Stir to mix.

5 TO 6 SERVINGS

CHICKEN SALAD WITH
MINTED YOGURT DRESSING

We've found yogurt to be a fine ingredient especially if it is a top-quality brand. Serve this light salad with bread sticks or crusty French rolls.

3/4 pound cooked skinless, boneless chicken breast
1/2 medium red onion
 1 medium cucumber
 1 cup low-fat or nonfat plain yogurt
1/3 cup chopped fresh mint, plus mint sprigs for garnish
    Salt and freshly ground pepper

1. Cut the chicken into 1/2- to 3/4-inch pieces. Coarsely chop the onion. Peel the cucumber if it is waxed, then cut it in half lengthwise. Scoop out the seeds and thinly slice or coarsely chop the cucumber halves.

2. In a medium mixing bowl, stir together the yogurt and chopped mint. Stir in the chicken, onion and cucumber. Season with salt and pepper to taste.

4 SERVINGS

CHICKEN AND ORANGE SALAD WITH CUMIN-YOGURT DRESSING

Citrus fruit is a wonderful ingredient. You can use the grated zest, juice and the fruit itself, as we have done in this recipe. Cornbread makes a delicious accompaniment.

$^3/_4$ pound cooked skinless, boneless chicken breast
 2 seedless oranges
 1 large bunch of green onions
 1 cup plain low-fat or nonfat yogurt
 2 teaspoons ground cumin
   Salt and freshly ground pepper

1. Cut the chicken into $^1/_2$- to $^3/_4$-inch pieces. Grate 2 teaspoons zest and squeeze 2 tablespoons juice from $^1/_2$ orange. Cut sections from the remaining $1^1/_2$ oranges. Thinly slice the green onions.

2. In a medium mixing bowl, stir together the yogurt, cumin, orange juice and orange zest. Add the chicken, green onion and orange segments. Stir to mix. Season with salt and pepper to taste.

3 TO 4 SERVINGS

ORZO CHICKEN SALAD

Orzo is a rice-shaped pasta that is popular in Greece. It is easy to eat on a fork and works beautifully in this colorful salad, which can be served warm or at room temperature. Fresh broccoli florets are commonly available all cut up and ready to cook in the produce or salad bar section of many supermarkets.

1 pound skinless, boneless chicken breasts
2 medium red bell peppers
1 cup orzo
3 cups broccoli florets
1 cup red wine vinaigrette salad dressing
   Salt and freshly ground pepper

1. Bring a large saucepan of salted water to a boil. Cut the chicken into 1-inch pieces. Cut the bell peppers into thin strips.

2. Add the orzo to the boiling water and cook 7 minutes. Add the broccoli and cook until the pasta is tender but still firm and the broccoli is crisp-tender, about 2 minutes longer; drain.

3. While the orzo is cooking, heat ½ cup of the vinaigrette in a large nonreactive frying pan. Add the chicken and cook, stirring often, until white but still juicy in the center, 5 to 7 minutes. (Most of the vinaigrette will evaporate.)

4. In a large bowl, combine the chicken and all the pan drippings with the orzo, broccoli and red peppers. Pour on the remaining ½ cup vinaigrette and toss. Season with salt and pepper to taste.

4 TO 5 SERVINGS

PARISIAN CHICKEN SALAD

This light and delicate chicken salad is flavored with tarragon, a favorite herb used in French cooking. Fresh tarragon is wonderful, but dried will do nicely, especially if you rub the leaves between your thumb and forefinger to release the oils. For a picture-pretty presentation, spoon the salad onto serving plates, then surround with Belgian endive spears and sliced radishes.

²/₃ cup slivered almonds
³/₄ pound cooked skinless, boneless chicken breast
  2 large celery ribs
³/₄ cup regular or low-fat mayonnaise
  3 tablespoons chopped fresh tarragon, or 2 teaspoons dried,
    plus additional fresh sprigs for garnish
    Salt and freshly ground pepper

1. Toast the almonds either in a microwave oven on High for about 3 minutes, stirring often, or on a baking sheet in a 350 degree F. oven for about 5 minutes, stirring often. Cut the chicken into ½- to ¾-inch pieces. Thinly slice the celery.

2. In a medium mixing bowl, stir together the mayonnaise and tarragon, then mix in ½ cup of the almonds, the chicken and the celery. Season with salt and pepper to taste.

3. Serve the chicken salad garnished with the remaining toasted almonds and fresh tarragon sprigs, if you have them.

3 TO 4 SERVINGS

SMOKED CHICKEN PESTO SALAD

Save this sophisticated salad as a first course or take it along on a picnic. For a complete menu, start with some fresh mozzarella and roasted peppers. Accompany the salad with some good Italian bread; then end with a light lemon sorbet and some amaretti cookies. Smoked chicken is available from specialty markets, but the salad is also delicious with plain, cold barbecued or broiled chicken. To save time, ask the market to slice the chicken for you. The salad is delicious served on a bed of arugula.

       8 ounces rotelle or other spiral pasta
       3 cups fresh broccoli florets
    1½ pounds boneless smoked chicken
       1 pint small cherry tomatoes
     ¾ cup purchased pesto sauce

1. Cook the pasta in a large pot of boiling salted water until almost tender, about 7 minutes. Add the broccoli florets and cook until the pasta is tender but still firm and the broccoli is crisp-tender, about 2 minutes. Drain the pasta and broccoli into a colander and transfer to a large bowl.

2. While the pasta is cooking, thinly slice the chicken, each slice with some of the outer smoked edges. Remove the stem end and cut the cherry tomatoes in half if they seem large.

3. Add the chicken and tomatoes to the bowl with the pasta. Add the pesto sauce and toss to coat thoroughly. Serve the salad at room temperature.

6 TO 8 SERVINGS

SOUTHERN TEA ROOM CHICKEN SALAD

This salad is reminiscent of gentler and less hectic times when ladies (and even gentlemen) enjoyed leisurely lunches. Though most true tea rooms are long gone, the chicken salad is so good, it deserves to be part of a new lunch tradition. If you wish, serve the salad in leaf lettuce cups and accompany with corn muffins.

1¼ pounds cooked skinless, boneless chicken breast
2½ cups seedless grapes, green and red
1½ cups regular or low-fat mayonnaise
3 tablespoons raspberry or other fruit vinegar
1 cup broken pecan halves
Salt and freshly ground pepper

1. Cut the chicken into ½- to ¾-inch cubes. If the grapes are large, cut them in half.

2. In a medium mixing bowl, stir together the mayonnaise and vinegar until blended. Add the grapes, pecans and chicken to the mayonnaise and stir to blend. Season lightly with salt and generously with pepper.

5 TO 6 SERVINGS

CHICKEN TACO SALAD

For a colorful party buffet, serve this salad with bowls of condiments, such as black olives, sliced pickled jalapeños, shredded lettuce and chopped tomato, on the side.

1½ pounds cooked skinless, boneless chicken breast
   2 large bunches of green onions
   1 cup sour cream or plain yogurt
   1 cup chunky picante salsa
   8 cups tortilla chips, or 12 to 16 taco shells

1. Cut the chicken into ½- to ¾-inch pieces. Thinly slice the green onions.

2. In a medium mixing bowl, stir together the sour cream and salsa until well blended. Add the chicken and 1 cup of the green onions. Toss to mix.

3. If using tortilla chips, make a bed of chips on a large platter, then spoon the salad in the center. If using taco shells, spoon the salad into the shells. Sprinkle the remaining green onions on top.

6 TO 8 SERVINGS

TOMATOES FILLED WITH BLUE CHEESE CHICKEN SALAD

Use ripe but firm tomatoes for this height-of-summer salad. Serve as a first course or light luncheon dish.

  4 medium tomatoes
     Salt and freshly ground pepper
³/₄ pound cooked skinless, boneless chicken breast
  2 large celery ribs
³/₄ cup chunky blue cheese salad dressing
¹/₂ cup herb-seasoned croutons

1. Cut a slice off the stem end of each tomato. Then use a grapefruit spoon to hollow out the inside, scooping out the pulp and seeds from each tomato. Use paper towels to dry the insides of the tomatoes, then season with salt and pepper. Invert onto paper towels to drain.

2. Cut the chicken into ¹/₂-inch pieces. Finely chop the celery. In a medium mixing bowl, mix the chicken, celery and blue cheese dressing. Season to taste with pepper. (If the dressing is very thick, add up to 1 tablespoon of water to thin to desired consistency.)

3. Just before serving, spoon the salad into the tomato halves. Sprinkle the croutons on top.

4 SERVINGS

CHICKEN WALDORF SALAD

Waldorf salad was created in the nineteenth century at the famous New York City hotel. Here it is streamlined and updated to become a main course for a light early autumn meal, when apples are at their best. Choose a crisp, bright red-skinned variety, such as red Delicious, for the prettiest color and best flavor.

3/4 pound skinless, boneless chicken breasts
1 large red-skinned apple
2 celery ribs
3/4 cup walnut pieces
1 cup regular or low-fat mayonnaise
  Salt and freshly ground pepper

1. Preheat the oven to 350 degrees F. Bring a large saucepan of salted water to a simmer. Cut the chicken into 1/2-inch cubes. Core the apple but leave the peel on. Cut the apple into 1/2-inch dice. Cut the celery into 1/2-inch pieces.

2. Add the chicken to the simmering water, cover and cook until white but still juicy in the center, 5 to 7 minutes. Drain into a colander. Let cool a minute or two, then pat dry on paper towels.

3. Meanwhile, spread out the walnuts on a small baking sheet and toast in the preheated oven about 5 minutes, until fragrant and very lightly browned. Immediately transfer to a plate to cool.

4. In a medium bowl, combine the chicken, toasted walnuts, apples and celery. Toss lightly. Add the mayonnaise and toss until evenly mixed. Season with salt and pepper to taste.

4 SERVINGS

8 PIZZAS, TORTILLAS AND HOT SANDWICHES

Sandwiches are so much a part of our food culture that we have taken the liberty of believing that you already know a good bit about them. Consequently, we haven't given space to the obvious traditional chicken sandwich with mayo and lettuce on white bread, or the quintessential chicken salad on whole wheat. Instead, we've given a contemporary spin to favorite themes and dreamed up some altogether new ideas for chicken-based sandwiches—many of which use pitas, pizza shells and tortillas in place of the usual bread.

Taking some liberties, we have borrowed "sandwiches" from many regions of our country: tortilla-based Chicken Fajitas from the Southwest, Chicken and Avocado Melt that fairly shouts California cooking and Shenandoah Chicken Sandwiches from the mid-South, as well as a Hot Chicken and Pepper Grinder from the Northeast. We also interpreted and streamlined sandwiches from some other countries. There is a Pizza Niçoise and an English Rarebit Chicken Melt, as well as a Neapolitan Chicken Pizza and Greek Pita Pizzas. Some of these sandwiches start with cooking the chicken while others make good use of leftover cooked chicken, but all deliver far more in taste satisfaction than the sum of the five ingredients that make them up.

ALPINE CHICKEN MELT

This sandwich is also wonderful with ham and Cheddar cheese, but the Canadian bacon makes it special. Also, it is the perfect size for the English muffins. Accompany with a salad of bitter greens and a creamy dressing.

10 ounces thinly sliced chicken cutlets
    Freshly ground pepper
 4 whole wheat English muffins
 4 tablespoons butter
 3 ounces thinly sliced Canadian bacon
 4 ounces thinly sliced or shredded Gruyère or Swiss cheese

1. Preheat the broiler. Season the chicken with pepper. Split the English muffins.

2. Heat the butter in a large frying pan. Add the chicken and the Canadian bacon and cook over medium-high heat for about 2 minutes per side, until the chicken is white but still moist in the center and the chicken and the bacon are golden.

3. Remove the chicken and bacon from the pan and brush the cut sides of the English muffins with the pan drippings. Layer with the Canadian bacon, then the chicken and finally the cheese.

4. Broil about 5 inches from the heat for 2 minutes, or until the edges of the English muffins are browned and crisp and the cheese is melted and bubbly.

4 SERVINGS

ARIZONA TORTILLA PIZZA

If you can't get the large 10- or 12-inch Sonora-style flour tortillas, simply use eight 7-inch tortillas. These "pizzas" are wonderful as a snack or as an informal supper. Serve corn on the cob and a salad of spinach and tropical fruits along with the pizzas.

3/4 pound cooked skinless, boneless chicken breasts
   Salt and freshly ground pepper
2 medium tomatoes
1 large bunch of green onions
4 flour tortillas, 10 to 12 inches in diameter
2 cups Monterey Jack cheese with hot chiles (8 ounces)

1. Preheat the oven to 500 degrees F. Thinly slice or shred the chicken across the grain. Season with salt and pepper to taste. Thinly slice the tomatoes. Thinly slice the green onions. Arrange layers of the chicken, tomato slices and green onions atop each tortilla. Sprinkle the cheese evenly on top.

2. Bake the pizzas in the upper third of the oven until the edges are crisp and lightly browned and the cheese is melted and bubbly, 5 to 7 minutes.

3. Use a pizza cutter or sharp knife to cut the pizzas into wedges to serve.

4 SERVINGS

CHICKEN AND AVOCADO MELT

This is a lovely sandwich to make when you have a ripe avocado on the counter. Here's a tip on peeling and pitting avocados in no time: Slit the avocado lengthwise in half right down to the pit. Twist, and the halves will come apart. Remove the pit. Slip an avocado skinner, a grapefruit knife or a large spoon between the avocado and skin and run it around the edge to remove each avocado half in one piece.

3/4 pound cooked skinless, boneless chicken breast
    Salt and freshly ground pepper
 1 large avocado
 8 slices of cracked wheat bread
1/2 cup bottled Russian or Thousand Island salad dressing
 1 cup shredded Monterey Jack cheese (4 ounces)

1. Preheat the broiler. Thinly slice the chicken and season with salt and pepper to taste. Peel, pit and thinly slice the avocado. Lightly toast the bread in a toaster.

2. Place the toasted bread on a baking sheet. Spread 1 tablespoon of the Russian dressing over each slice. Top with the chicken and then the avocado slices. Sprinkle the cheese on top.

3. Broil about 5 inches from the heat for 2 minutes, until the sandwich is heated through and the cheese is melted and bubbly.

4 SERVINGS

CHICKEN AND BEAN QUESADILLAS

Quesadillas are usually lightly filled tortillas that are folded and grilled, then served as a snack. To make them heartier, we have devised a baking method that sandwiches two tortillas over and under a generous mound of refried beans, chicken and cheese. Add an avocado salad and you have a complete meal in no time.

3/4 pound cooked skinless, boneless chicken breast
   Salt and freshly ground pepper
1 can (16 ounces) refried beans
8 flour tortillas, 7 to 8 inches in diameter
2 cups shredded Monterey Jack cheese (8 ounces)
1 1/2 cups bottled red or green salsa

1. Preheat the oven to 450 degrees F. Thinly slice or shred the chicken across the grain. Season lightly with salt and pepper. Spread 1/4 cup of the refried beans over each of the tortillas.

2. On a baking sheet, place 4 tortillas, bean side up. Sprinkle with the chicken and half the cheese. Cover with the remaining tortillas, bean side down, and press lightly on the edges.

3. Bake for 5 minutes, sprinkle the remaining cheese on top and bake 3 to 5 minutes longer, until the cheese is melted and the tortillas are thoroughly warmed.

4. To serve, use a pizza cutter or sharp knife to cut each quesadilla into 4 wedges.

4 SERVINGS

CHICKEN AND BROCCOLI PIZZAS

This is a nontraditional, but definitely delicious pizza. Depending upon the season, you could substitute lots of other vegetables such as asparagus or snow peas or even cooked Brussels sprouts! Broccoli florets are usually available cut and ready to cook from the supermarket salad bar or produce section. Serve the pizza with sliced tomatoes drizzled with a vinaigrette.

3/4 pound thinly sliced chicken cutlets
   Salt and freshly ground pepper
3/4 cup extra virgin olive oil
 2 cups fresh or frozen broccoli florets
 4 individual pizza bread shells (two 8-ounce packages)
 1 cup shredded or thinly sliced Swiss cheese (4 ounces)

1. Preheat the oven to 500 degrees F. Season the chicken lightly with salt and generously with pepper, then cut the chicken into thin crosswise slices.

2. Heat the oil in a large frying pan, then sauté the chicken and broccoli over medium-high heat, stirring constantly, until the chicken is white throughout and the broccoli is crisp-tender, 2 to 3 minutes. Brush the bread shells with some of the pan drippings, then arrange the chicken and broccoli to within 3/4 inch of the edges. Drizzle with any remaining pan drippings, then cover with the cheese.

3. Bake the pizzas for 5 to 7 minutes until the crusts are golden brown with crisped edges and the cheese is melted.

4 SERVINGS

DANISH CHICKEN MELT

There are several brands of mustard-mayonnaise sandwich sauce
to be found in the condiment section of most supermarkets. Try to
find one that is particularly zippy with good mustard. Round out
this simple sandwich supper with a dilled cucumber salad and
potato pancakes or hashed browns.

3/4 pound cooked skinless, boneless chicken breast
    Salt and freshly ground pepper
 1 medium sweet red onion
 4 ounces Fontina cheese, preferably Danish
 8 slices dark rye bread
 6 tablespoons mustard-mayonnaise sandwich sauce

1. Preheat the broiler. Thinly slice the chicken. Season lightly with
salt and generously with pepper. Thinly slice the onion. Thinly
slice the cheese. Lightly toast the bread in a toaster.

2. Place the toasted bread on a baking sheet. Spread the mustard-
mayonnaise sauce over the slices. Add the chicken, then some
onion slices and finally the cheese.

3. Broil about 5 inches from the heat for 2 minutes, or until the
sandwich is heated through and the cheese is melted and bubbly.

4 SERVINGS

ENGLISH RAREBIT CHICKEN MELT

Serve the open-faced sandwiches with a spinach salad and a tankard of ale.

³/₄ pound cooked skinless, boneless chicken breast
   Freshly ground pepper
4 English muffins
6 tablespoons mustard-mayonnaise sandwich sauce
2 medium tomatoes
1 cup shredded sharp Cheddar cheese (4 ounces)

1. Preheat the broiler. Thinly slice the chicken and season generously with pepper. Split the English muffins and spread the mustard-mayonnaise over the cut sides. Slice the tomatoes. Layer the English muffins with the chicken and then the tomatoes. Top with shredded cheese.

2. Set the sandwiches on a baking sheet. Broil about 5 inches from the heat source for 2 minutes, or until the edges of the English muffins are browned and crisp and the cheese is melted and bubbly.

4 SERVINGS

CHICKEN FAJITAS

Grilling imparts a wonderful smoky flavor, but you can simply broil the chicken or sauté it in a hot frying pan if you wish. Shredded cheese, chopped jalapeño peppers and sliced onions are all traditional garnishes for fajitas.

```
    1 pound thinly sliced chicken cutlets
      Salt and freshly ground pepper
    2 tablespoons vegetable oil
    8 flour tortillas, 7 to 8 inches in diameter
    1 cup prepared guacamole
1 1/2 cups bottled chunky red salsa
```

1. Light a medium-hot fire in a barbecue grill. Season the chicken lightly with salt and generously with pepper. Brush with the oil.

2. Grill the chicken a total of about 6 minutes, until nicely browned on the outside and white but still moist in the center. Remove from the grill, then slice or shred thinly across the grain.

3. While the chicken is cooking, wrap the tortillas in foil and heat for about 3 minutes on the grill or wrap in microwave-safe paper towels and heat on High for about 1 minute in a microwave oven.

4. Assemble the fajitas by arranging all ingredients at the table and allowing each person to make his or her own. Spread each tortilla with about 2 tablespoons of the guacamole, then spoon some of the chicken in the center. Add a little salsa and roll up to enclose the filling. Serve with remaining salsa on the side.

4 SERVINGS

GREEK PITA PIZZAS

Serve these simple, zesty pizzas with a tomato and cucumber salad and enjoy a piece of bakery baklava for dessert.

$1/2$ pound cooked skinless, boneless chicken breast
    Salt and freshly ground pepper
 3 teaspoons oregano
 3 tablespoons extra virgin olive oil
 3 pita breads, 6 inches in diameter
$3/4$ cup crumbled feta cheese (3 ounces)

1. Preheat the broiler. Coarsely dice or thinly slice the chicken across the grain. Season lightly with salt and generously with pepper and 2 teaspoons of the oregano. Stir the remaining oregano into the olive oil.

2. Split the pita breads into 6 thin rounds. Brush the cut sides with the oregano-flavored oil. Top with the chicken and then the feta cheese.

3. Broil the pizzas about 5 inches from the heat source for about 2 minutes, until the cheese is bubbly and the edges of the pita breads are browned and crisp. To serve, cut each pizza in half or in quarters.

2 TO 3 SERVINGS

HOT CHICKEN AND BISCUITS WITH GRAVY

This will remind you of Sunday dinner at Grandma's, except that the preparation takes mere minutes instead of all day. Complete the nostalgic picture with green beans and mashed potatoes. We've given you plenty of gravy.

1 pound thinly sliced chicken cutlets
1/2 teaspoon freshly ground pepper
4 tablespoons butter
1/4 cup all-purpose flour
3 cups chicken broth
    Salt
8 bakery baking powder biscuits

1. Season the chicken with the pepper. Heat the butter in a large frying pan. Add the chicken and cook over medium-high heat for 2 to 3 minutes, turning, until the chicken is light golden and white but still moist in center. With tongs, remove the chicken to a plate.

2. Stir the flour into the drippings in the skillet to make a paste. Cook, stirring, for 1 minute, until the paste is golden. Slowly whisk the broth into the flour mixture, then cook and stir over medium heat until the gravy thickens and boils for 1 minute. Season with salt and additional pepper to taste.

3. Split the biscuits and arrange the chicken on the bottom halves. Ladle some gravy over the chicken. Replace the tops of the biscuits and ladle more gravy over all.

4 SERVINGS

HOT CHICKEN AND PEPPER GRINDER

Whether you call this a grinder, a sub or a hero, we call it a darned good American sandwich. The traditional accompaniments are shredded iceberg lettuce and French fries.

3/4 pound cooked skinless, boneless chicken breast
1 large green bell pepper
2 cups chunky garden-style prepared pasta sauce
1 loaf (10 to 12 ounces) frozen garlic bread
6 ounces thinly sliced provolone cheese

1. Preheat the broiler. Thinly slice the chicken. Cut the green pepper into thin strips. Heat the spaghetti sauce in a nonreactive medium frying pan or saucepan. Add the bell pepper and simmer over medium-low heat until the pepper is softened, 5 minutes. Add the chicken and simmer for 1 minute longer.

2. While the pepper is simmering, slightly thaw the garlic bread in a microwave oven if necessary. Place the garlic bread, cut sides up, on a baking sheet. Broil about 5 inches from the heat for 2 minutes, or until golden and hot.

3. Place the garlic bread on serving plates. Layer half the garlic bread with the chicken mixture and sauce, then cover with the cheese and the remaining bread to make sandwiches. Eat with a knife and fork.

4 SERVINGS

CHICKEN NACHOS

Since it is practically guaranteed that every child (and adult) in America will happily eat nachos, why not turn this favorite munchy into a whole meal? Cook them either in the broiler or the microwave, then personalize the nachos by accompanying them with the usual sour cream (or plain yogurt), guacamole and salsa in the heat of your choice.

$\frac{1}{2}$ pound cooked skinless, boneless chicken breast
    Salt and freshly ground pepper
1 large bunch of green onions
3 cups corn tortilla chips
1$\frac{1}{2}$ cups (6 ounces) shredded Cheddar, Monterey Jack or taco
    cheese
1 can (2 ounces) sliced black olives (about $\frac{1}{2}$ cup)

1. Preheat the broiler if using. Shred or thinly slice the chicken across the grain. Season lightly with salt and pepper to taste. Thinly slice the green onions, including tops, to make about 1 cup.

2. Place the chicken in the center of a large ovenproof or microwave-safe platter. Surround with the tortilla chips. Sprinkle on the cheese, then the olives and green onions.

3. Broil about 5 inches from the heat for 2 minutes or heat in a microwave oven on High for 1$\frac{1}{2}$ minutes, or until the cheese is melted and bubbly.

2 TO 3 SERVINGS

NEAPOLITAN CHICKEN PIZZA

This is pizza as you know and love it, complete with chicken, of course. You can use prepared pizza sauce, but we prefer some of the better-quality thick spaghetti sauces, especially the ones flavored with basil. If you have leftover cooked chicken, shred and use it, brushing the pizza crusts with the olive oil.

³/₄ pound skinless, boneless chicken breasts
2 tablespoons extra virgin olive oil
1 cup prepared spaghetti or pizza sauce
4 individual pizza bread shells (two 8-ounce packages)
6 ounces shredded or thinly sliced mozzarella cheese
   (1¹/₂ cups)

1. Preheat the oven to 500 degrees F. Cut the chicken into 1-inch pieces. Heat the oil in a medium frying pan and sauté the chicken over medium-high heat, stirring almost constantly, until white throughout but still juicy, about 4 minutes.

2. Spread the pizza sauce on the bread shells to within ³/₄ inch of the edges. Add the chicken and juices, then the cheese.

3. Bake the pizzas for 5 to 7 minutes, until the crusts are golden brown with crisped edges and the cheese is melted.

4 SERVINGS

PIZZA NIÇOISE

Authentic Niçoise olives are very tiny and take too long to pit for our purposes, but be sure to use good-quality pitted black olives as a very fine substitute.

3/4 pound cooked skinless, boneless chicken breast
    Freshly ground pepper
1/2 pound plum tomatoes
1 loaf (10 to 12 ounces) frozen garlic bread
1/2 cup thinly sliced black olives
1 cup shredded or thinly sliced mozzarella cheese (4 ounces)

1. Preheat the broiler. Thinly slice the chicken and season with pepper to taste. Thinly slice the tomatoes. Slightly thaw the garlic bread in a microwave oven.

2. Place the garlic bread, cut sides up, on a baking sheet. Set under the broiler about 5 inches from the heat and broil about 1 minute, until golden. Remove from the oven; leave the broiler on.

3. Layer the chicken and then the tomatoes on the garlic bread. Sprinkle on the olives and top with the cheese.

4. Return to the broiler for about 1 1/2 minutes, until the cheese is melted and lightly tinged with brown. To serve, cut each pizza crosswise on the diagonal into 4 slices.

4 SERVINGS

CHICKEN PESTO PIZZA

Frozen or bottled pesto is a fabulous convenience product. Many supermarket delis and specialty food shops sell freshly prepared pesto in containers. Seasoned bread shells for pizza are relatively new. Here the two form a tasty basis for a memorable chicken pizza.

3/4 pound cooked skinless, boneless chicken breast
    Freshly ground pepper
1/2 pound plum tomatoes
 4 individual pizza bread shells (two 8-ounce packages)
1/2 cup pesto sauce
3/4 cup shredded mozzarella cheese (4 ounces)

1. Preheat the oven to 500 degrees F. Shred or thinly slice the chicken across the grain. Season with pepper to taste. Thinly slice the tomatoes.

2. Spread the bread shells with pesto sauce to within 3/4 inch of the edges. Layer with the tomatoes and then the chicken. Sprinkle the cheese on top.

3. Bake the pizzas for 5 to 7 minutes, until the crusts are golden brown with crisped edges and the cheese is melted.

4 SERVINGS

RIVIERA CHICKEN AND ROASTED PEPPER SANDWICH

These Mediterranean ingredients will transport you to the Riviera, at least for an hour or so. The heady flavors of fresh basil, garlic and roasted peppers make a wonderful sandwich. Add chicken, and the meal is complete.

3/4 pound cooked, skinless boneless chicken breast
    Salt and freshly ground pepper
1 loaf (10 to 12 ounces) frozen garlic bread
1 jar (7 1/2 ounces) roasted red peppers
3/4 cup loosely packed fresh basil leaves
6 ounces sliced provolone cheese

1. Preheat the broiler. Thinly slice the chicken. Season lightly with salt and generously with pepper. Thaw the garlic bread slightly in a microwave oven.

2. Place the garlic bread, cut sides up, on a baking sheet. Set under the broiler about 5 inches from the heat, for about 1 minute, or until golden. Remove from the oven; leave the broiler on.

3. Arrange the chicken over the bread. Add a layer of the peppers and sprinkle half the basil leaves on top of the peppers. Cover with the cheese slices. Return to the broiler for about 1 minute, until the cheese is melted and lightly tinged with gold. To serve, cut each bread on the diagonal into 4 pieces. Garnish each with the remaining 1/4 cup basil leaves.

4 SERVINGS

SHENANDOAH CHICKEN SANDWICHES

The inspiration for this sandwich comes from much time spent in the beautiful Shenandoah Valley, where greens cooked with bacon and vinegar are a regional specialty. We like it with collards, but you can use whatever fresh (or frozen) greens are easily available.

3/4 pound thinly sliced chicken cutlets
   Freshly ground pepper
6 slices of bacon
1/2 pound collard greens
2 tablespoons cider vinegar
4 large seeded sandwich rolls, such as Kaiser rolls

1. Season the chicken generously with pepper. Cut into strips about 1½ inches long and ½ inch wide. Cut the bacon into 1-inch pieces. Discard the tough collard stems; thinly slice the leaves.

2. In a large frying pan, cook the bacon over medium heat until about half cooked, 2 to 3 minutes. Add the chicken to the pan and fry, stirring often, until the bacon is crisp and the chicken is white in center, about 3 minutes.

3. Add the collards to the pan and cook, stirring, until the greens are almost wilted, about 1 minute. Add the vinegar and cook, stirring, for 30 seconds.

4. To serve, split the rolls in half. Ladle the hot chicken mixture into the sandwich rolls and serve at once.

4 SERVINGS

CHICKEN SLOPPY JOES

Just like the old favorite, but made new with chicken. Use a good-quality bottled chunky tomato sauce with lots of onion and green pepper. Then garnish the sandwich as you wish—shredded lettuce and/or Cheddar cheese are typical choices. Buy the chicken already ground or do it yourself in a food processor, as directed in step 1.

1 pound skinless, boneless chicken breasts
  Salt and freshly ground pepper
2 tablespoons olive oil
2 cups prepared chunky garden-style pasta sauce
2 tablespoons red wine vinegar
4 large, soft sandwich buns

1. Cut the chicken into 1-inch pieces and pulse in a food processor until coarsely ground. Season lightly with salt and generously with pepper.

2. Heat the oil in a large frying pan. Add the chicken and cook, over medium-high heat, until white throughout. Stir in the pasta sauce and vinegar. Bring to a boil, reduce the heat to medium-low and simmer for 4 minutes. Season with salt and pepper to taste.

3. Split the sandwich buns in half. Ladle the hot chicken mixture into the buns.

4 SERVINGS

SUN-DRIED TOMATO AND GOAT CHEESE PIZZA

This is an adult pizza, especially well suited to a salad of arugula tossed with a balsamic vinaigrette. Cut into thinner slices, these pizzas make excellent hot hors d'oeuvres.

$3/4$ pound cooked skinless, boneless chicken breast
   Freshly ground pepper
 1 loaf (10 to 12 ounces) French bread
$1/2$ cup sun-dried tomatoes in oil, plus $1/4$ cup of the oil
 6 ounces mild goat cheese
$1/2$ cup chopped fresh basil or parsley

1. Preheat the broiler. Thinly slice the chicken and season it with pepper. Cut the loaf of bread horizontally in half. Thinly slice or chop the sun-dried tomatoes.

2. Brush the cut sides of the bread with the oil from the tomatoes and place, cut sides up, on a baking sheet. Arrange the chicken on the bread and crumble the cheese on top. Sprinkle all but about 2 tablespoons of the parsley over the cheese.

3. Broil about 4 inches from the heat for about 2 minutes, until the cheese is melted and the edges of the bread are browned.

4. To serve, sprinkle with the remaining 2 tablespoons chopped parsley over the tops. Cut the bread halves into 4 diagonal slices each and serve open-faced.

4 SERVINGS

CHICKEN TACOS AS YOU LIKE THEM

Choose among mild, medium or hot chunky salsas. There are dozens of brands available, each with a different personality.

1 pound skinless, boneless chicken breasts
   Salt and freshly ground pepper
1 small head of iceberg lettuce
8 taco shells
2 cups shredded Monterey Jack, Cheddar or taco cheese
   (8 ounces)
1½ cups bottled chunky red salsa

1. Bring a medium saucepan of salted water to a boil over high heat. Meanwhile, cut the chicken into thin strips. Add to water, reduce the heat to a simmer and cook until the chicken is tender and just white throughout, 5 to 7 minutes; drain. Season the chicken with salt and pepper to taste.

2. While the chicken is cooking, shred the lettuce.

3. Divide the chicken filling among the taco shells. Garnish with the cheese and salsa and top with the shredded lettuce.

4 SERVINGS

INDEX